Copyright © 2007 Word of Mouth Travels
Editors and Writers: Claudia Monteiro and Owen O'Leary

Book Design and Cover by Claire Dowling

Portraits and Photography by Matthew James Reid,
except those on pages 2, 30, 74, 111, 117 (© Claire Dowling);
15 (© Stewart Hardy); 26 (© David Ross); 35 (© David Harding);
68 (© Rachel Cowan); Paul Davidson (© 71, 130); 79 (© Lindsay Perth)
Poem 'Scotland' © Alastair Reid
Illustration Copyright © 2007 Mina Braun (pg 107) and © Paula Kennedy (pg 103)

First published in Great Britain in November 2007 by Word of Mouth Travels Ltd
19 Tylers Acre Avenue
Edinburgh EH12 7JE
www.wordofmouthtravels.co.uk

ISBN 978-0-9557529-0-2

Word of Mouth Travels books are available at special discounts when purchased in bulk.
Special editions or book excerpts can also be created to specification.
For details check our website www.wordofmouthtravels.co.uk

You can buy the book online at www.amazon.co.uk or from our website
www.localsguidetoedinburgh.com

Still reading this? Come on, there's a whole city waiting for you. Get stuck in!

The Locals Guide to
Edinburgh

word of mouth travels

2008 - 2009

URBAN PO
PROJEC

START SPRE

POETR
ON
THE STR

Contents

Welcome 4
What this book is about 7
Walking Map **8**
Neighbourhoods 10

Where to Stay 12
Being from Edinburgh 26
Scots for Weather **2**7

All You Can Eat **32**
One Recipe 60
Two Films, Two Books 61

Beautiful Walks 62
Cold Comforts 72

Drink & Be Merry 76
You Should be Dancing, Yeah 96
Festival Fever **100**
One Poem 103
Off the Beaten Attractions 104

What's in Stores? 108
Romantic Edinburgh 128
No Money, Old Money 132

The Locals' Directory *134*
Thank You All 138
Too Good to Leave Out 141

The New
Town

CRESCENT

A CASTLE slap BANG

in the middle of the city

A labyrinth of narrow steps & alleyways

Close your eyes. Imagine the hustle and bustle of an ancient capital four hundred years ago. Cobbled streets, a maze of wynds and closes. The North Sea and Firth of Forth open up in front of your eyes from the top of the city's seven hills. Edinburgh's majestic volcanic rock, Arthur's Seat, stands firm demanding your attention. Nature is everywhere.

Crisp and clear winter mornings. Cold nights in cosy fire-lit pubs. Festival revellers going to bed as the sun rises on the horizon. Students soaking up the sun on the Meadows' green grass. The sound of bagpipes blasting out of ginger haired, tartan-trimmed souvenir shops.

Edinburgh, a city of two halves: Old Town and New, underground vaults lurking beneath towering tenements, a place of dark and light, the spiritual home of Dr Jekyll and Mr Hyde. Blooming gardens in elegant New Town crescents. The weather-beaten contrast of Leith Docks. Lawyers and financiers meet in the finest eateries while drunken comrades share stories on the city's park benches.

Edinburgh is neither a city nor a town. Perhaps it's a small city, maybe it's a big town populated by small villages. A cosmopolitan capital, yet strict in keeping at bay the stress and clutter that turns other cities into urban jungles. A place where your friends are no more than half an hour away; where the pub is a cycle down (or if you're unlucky) up the hill, where walking to work is a delightful stroll through architectural treasures.

It is the city of storytellers and ghost tours, the literary home of both modern day best-selling authors and classic writers of the past. Nearly three centuries since Edinburgh became the focus of the Scottish Enlightenment, locals still enjoy getting together in clubs and societies to debate their favourite topics and revive local traditions (with the aid of some alcoholic encouragement). It is the place of inventors, thinkers, artists and home to the greatest summer festivals in the world.

Edinburgh grabs you and won't let go. Just give in.

What this book is about

We've asked everyone we know in Edinburgh to tell us exactly what makes home special; which eateries, bars, shops and walks they absolutely couldn't live without. And then we asked some more. We invited local legends to guide you through the city, and they'll be speaking directly to you from the pages of this book. Whether you're a visitor who does not want to do the 'tourist trail', or a local resident who is willing to try some new things, take their word for it and check out their stories, tips and thoughts.

Welcome to Edinburgh, you've arrived...

p.s. – We have a no advertising policy. Instead, places are featured on merit alone, either because they're unique, inspiring or run by people who genuinely care about their trade. This book has been written, designed and photographed by Edinburgh-based folk and printed in Scotland.

~~~~ 100% ~~~~
Made in Scotland

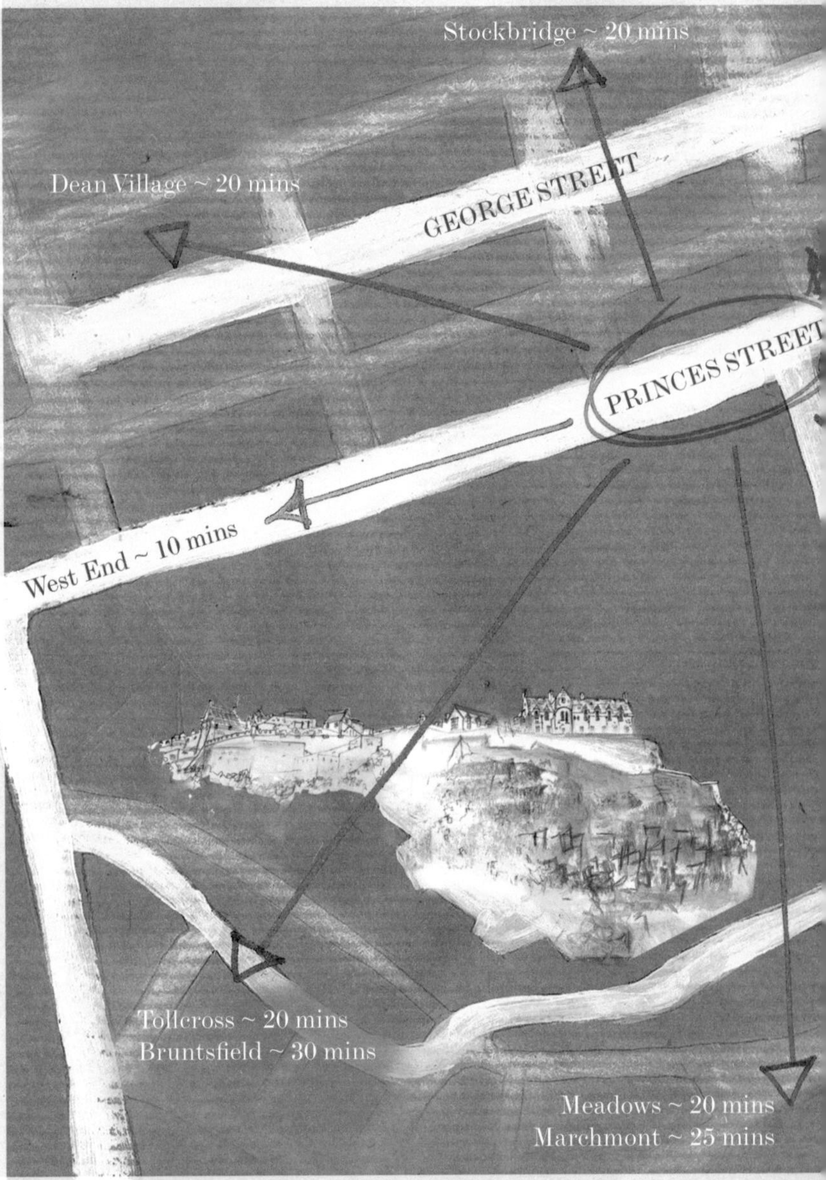

Stockbridge ~ 20 mins

Dean Village ~ 20 mins

GEORGE STREET

PRINCES STREET

West End ~ 10 mins

Tollcross ~ 20 mins
Bruntsfield ~ 30 mins

Meadows ~ 20 mins
Marchmont ~ 25 mins

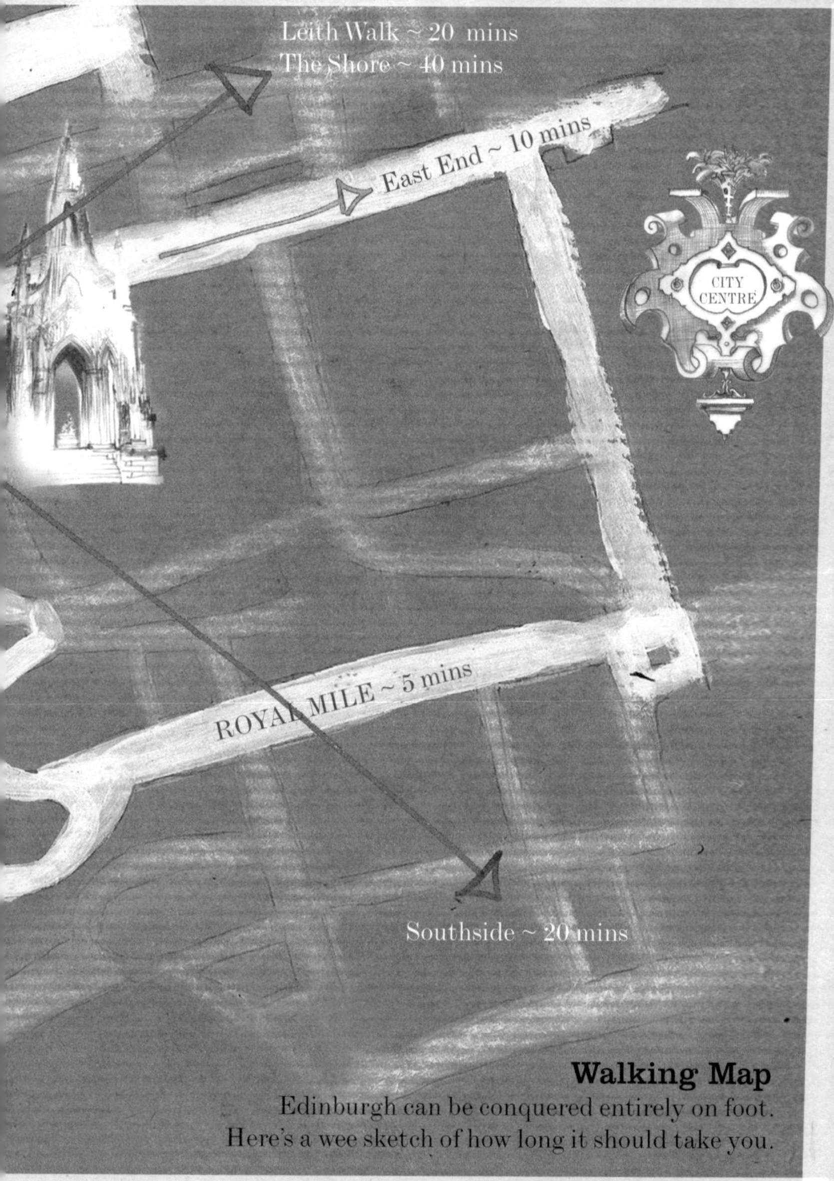

Leith Walk ~ 20 mins
The Shore ~ 40 mins

East End ~ 10 mins

CITY
CENTRE

ROYAL MILE ~ 5 mins

Southside ~ 20 mins

Walking Map
Edinburgh can be conquered entirely on foot.
Here's a wee sketch of how long it should take you.

Neighbourhoods
A few words about a few places

Stockbridge

If Stockbridge was a day of the week it would be a Sunday. Just a stone's throw from Princes Street, Georgian elegance mixes with a country village vibe as its streets are lined with small curious shops, cheesemongers, butchers, bakeries and a clutch of delis to serve this affluent part of town. Head to Glenogle Road and check out the Colonies, charming low-cost housing built in the 19th century for the city's tradespeople. To see how the how the other half lives wander along Ann Street, often referred to as Edinburgh's prettiest street. With the expanse of Inverleith Park at its edge, the Royal Botanic Gardens nearby and the Water of Leith running throughout, Stockbridge is an ideal place to unwind as everything slows down just a little bit.

Old Town

The Old Town sits on a dramatic volcanic spinal ridge. The Royal Mile, the thoroughfare that connects the Castle to Holyrood Palace and the new Scottish Parliament, has been Edinburgh's hub since it became a town, back in the 12th century. Ancient history and medieval architecture populate the cobbled wynds and closes dotted around the Mile. This is the home of gothic gore, ghost sighting tours, haunted underground vaults and the obligatory tourist tat shops and visitors' attractions. Imposing views of the sea to the east, the sight of the New Town and the Firth of Forth to the north. To the south (heading to South Bridge, Nicolson Street and Clerk Street), lies a mix of University buildings, student cafés, charity shops and cheap ethnic eateries.

New Town

Famously designed by 20-year-old architect James Craig in 1766, the New Town is a rational and planned exercise in geometry with Georgian terraces and elegant Neoclassical details, stretching north of Princes Street. Its crescents, circuses and squares are dotted with pristine private gardens, luxury cars and the occasional well-to-do student popping out in their pyjamas for a pint of milk. It is a relatively quiet neighbourhood with grandiose windows framed by spacious apartments, and the place to go for expensive antique shops, bespoke services and understated but beautiful boutique hotels.

Leith

Leith is only a song in a taxi ride away from the heart of Edinburgh. Once Scotland's main port and a town in its own right, Leith's economy used to gravitate around all things maritime. Irvine Welsh famously depicted the area's social meltdown in the best-selling novel Trainspotting, but nowadays places like the Shore sport the neighbourhood's arrival in the 21st century: flash new pads sit next to social housing, Michelin star restaurants co-exist with greasy spoon cafés, and merry locals share watering holes with young professionals. Leith Walk has probably got the highest number of traditional barbers and bargain stores anywhere in Edinburgh.

Bruntsfield & Morningside

Following in the footsteps of the upwardly mobile, these two neighbourhoods flow into each other. Historically known as Burgh Muir, a quarter for Edinburgh's plague victims, Bruntsfield has never been in better health. Emerging from Tollcross, scruffy charm gives way to bijoux boutiques, delis and cafés as affluent students and young professionals enjoy the park side benefits of being next to Bruntsfield Links and the Meadows. The main street naturally descends into Morningside, home to millionaires and a by word for Edinburgh's conservative character. The neighbourhood is less old money than it once was but still retains an image that's a class apart.

WHERE

TO STAY

"When we were growing up we were lucky to have a holiday. We walked all the way to Edinburgh and stayed in a shed near Holyrood Park."

"A shed! We were blessed to find a bridge to shelter under on the Cowgate avoiding the sideways rain."

"A bridge! My folks took us stargazing on Calton Hill every night and if it rained we had to count the drops until we passed out."

"Ah the joys of the great outdoors. We had to find a sewer under the Royal Mile that was so bad even the rats couldn't bear it!"

There's no need to try and outdo Monty Python's Four Yorkshiremen. Instead choose from our stayover shortlist selection. Across all types and tastes here's our top spots...

■The Witchery ■Belford Hostel ■The Glasshouse

Budget accommodation without budging on standards.

The benchmark by which all other hostels will be judged can be found at **Edinburgh Central**. Open since 2006, all contemporary rooms are ensuite, have keycard entry, disabled access and range from single, twin and eight bedded options. A stone's throw from Princes St – this hostel has it all (9 Haddington Pl, top of Leith Walk, t: 0131 524 2090, Map A2).

At the converted 19th century Gothic church that is the **Belford Hostel**, dorm guests get to sleep under a vaulted ceiling and beautiful stained glass windows. With just partition walls dividing the dorms this can be more noisy than most hostels but the friendly, lively atmosphere here is one of Belford's greatest assets. Private rooms are quieter, and the vibrant bar and outdoor BBQ space makes for a sociable stay (6/8 Douglas Gardens, West End/Dean Village, t: 131 220 2200, beyond Map D4).

B&B should never stand for boring and bland but too often it does. Steer clear of the mundane and go for these braw* and barry** options!

Six Mary's Place is No.1 in countless guesthouse polls and is tops for us too. Why? Georgian elegance meets contemporary comfort in this Stockbridge treasure. Not only that but a reputation for excellent service, a vegetarian breakfast the envy of many a meat eater and a tranquil suntrap garden to make the most of the Scottish sun. Make Six Mary's Place your place too (Raeburn Pl, Stockbridge, t: 0131 332 8965, Map D3).

A short walk from Salisbury Crags and Arthur's Seat, affordable luxury awaits guests of **Aonach Mor Guest House**, a family run Victorian house. Despite such high standards there's a relaxed, informal atmosphere that perfectly captures the home from home effect. Guests staying in the Jacobean Four Poster bedroom with en suite steam room will want to move in for good! (14 Kilmaurs Terrace, Newington, t: 0131 667 8694, beyond Map A7)

*fine, splendid   **good, wonderful

INTERVIEW:
Tim Bell

(tour guide & seafarers' chaplain
to the Port of Leith)

In the 1980s Tim swapped his native Northumberland for
Leith, the Edinburgh harbour behind the cult hit-film of
the 1990s, Trainspotting (based on Irvine Welsh's novel).
He's a converted Leither - it's the sense of being in a community that really draws him to the place. One day Tim
received an email from a Dutch journalist asking where
the Trainspotting tour was. It didn't exist. And that's
when he decided to start one.

66 A lot of people saw the film but had no contact with the
book, and don't even realise that the story was set in Leith. You
see, the book is all about a generation that was lost to drugs in
Leith in the 1980s, during Thatcher's Britain, whereas the film
was shot in different locations in Scotland and the mood is party
time in the 1990s. The declining Leith Docks left an easy point
of ingress to the Scottish mainland for the drug smugglers and
there is a whole generation of runners who became ghosts. Irvine
Welsh was working in the Housing Department at the time and
captured all those stories.

Everything has changed now, of course, and there are fewer and
fewer ships coming to Leith. As a chaplain I take personal interest
in the sailors, some of whom are away from home on brutally long
contracts. They come from all over the world: Russia, Ukraine,
the Philippines, Cape Verde. I take them to Calton Hill so they
can get a good view of the city; if they are fit men I take them
hiking up Arthur's Seat instead.

For a well earned pint I'll take the sailors to The Port O' Leith
Bar. Mary Moriarty, the landlady, is known as The Queen of

Choose a family.
Choose a career.
...cars,

Tim on Leith docks

Leith and has been running the place for more than 20 years. She has a great sense of community and makes the point of introducing people to each other at the bar. It's a regulars' pub where you can have a millionaire drinking next to someone who has just cashed their unemployment cheque. Even Hollywood actor Christian Slater stopped by when he was in town.

Because Leith has such strong ties with the sea, Trinity House Maritime Museum is a wonderful place to visit. It guards this incredible amount of maritime memorabilia, so much of it related to the history of Leith. Located in a beautiful 19th century Georgian house it was founded by the Incorporation of Masters and Mariners, an organisation created in the 14th century to provide welfare to the seafarers' families – so far ahead of its time!

And I would always recommend people to walk around the medieval streets of Leith (between the Shore, Bernard Street and Constitution Street). You get a real sense for how all those buildings are pieced together in what was once a bustling harbour!"

See The Locals' Directory on page 134 for Tim's top tips.
To book Tim Bell's Trainspotting Tours go to www.leithwalks.co.uk
or t: 07803 051 093.

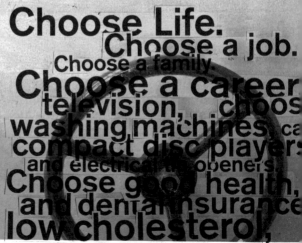

Choose Life. Choose a job. Choose a family. Choose a career television, choos washing machines ca compact disc player and electrical tin openers. Choose good health, and dental insurance low cholesterol,

Stay stylish in surrounds that bring old Edinburgh bang up to date...

A former Seaman's Mission at Leith docks is now the divine **Malmaison Hotel Edinburgh**. Sleek and chic, this hotel is a designer's dream. Feel like Alice in Wonderland amongst the oversized furniture and whether you have a Cheshire cat or 101 Dalmatians your pets will get the five-star treatment too (1 Tower Pl, Leith, t: 0131 468 5000, beyond Map A1).

Perfectly capturing the duality of Edinburgh's old and new, **The Glasshouse** marries style and substance for a unique boutique experience. Fronted by the façade of the 150 year old Lady Glenorchy church, the hotel blends clean lines and contemporary luxury with its old world entrance. The two acre lavender scented rooftop garden overlooking Calton Hill allows you to enjoy that breath of fresh air that comes with staying here (2 Greenside Pl, New Town, t: 0131 525 8200, Map A3).

Go back in time and wake up surrounded by history. These are the experiences you will never forget...

Fall under the spell of **The Witchery**. One of the most talked about establishments in the entire city will leave you speechless upon entering. Royal gothic suites in deep rich colours, lavishly decorated with antiques, exude decadence. Four-poster beds, fresco ceilings, private libraries and rolltop baths big enough for two are just the tip of the iceberg. Ravishing. Opulent. Magical. A renaissance painting brought to life (Castlehill, Royal Mile, t: 0131 225 5613, Map B4).

Step into the land of Shackleton in **Channings**. Formerly the home of the great Antarctic explorer, this town house hotel has the feel of a private members club in the bar and restaurant. The striking deluxe rooms with Shackleton prints, stand-alone baths and underfloor heating are there to be discovered (12-16 South Learmonth Gardens, Comely Bank, t: 0131 274 7401, beyond Map D3).

Malcolm Fraser has always been interested in people's roots and sense of place which is fortunate, because his job seems to deal with so much of that.

His favourite projects come in the shape of buildings that engage with the old but are not necessarily old in themselves. In his view, architecture is about seeking light and a spiritual relationship with the landscape, allowing the great views of the outside to flood into buildings. To find out what Malcolm means take a stroll around some of his award-winning cultural buildings: Dance Base, the Scottish Poetry Library and The Scottish Storytelling Centre.

What is really important is this tension between dark and light, the duality that constantly permeates through the city. Edinburgh is the home of Dr Jekyll and Mr Hyde, the landscape of mountains and valleys, the site where extremes meet. And that carries on through to literature: on the one hand you have Irvine Welsh with those dark stories of Leith and on the other McCall Smith and his more genteel stories.

INTERVIEW:
Malcolm Fraser

Malcolm at Bennets Bar

Edinburgh was one of the most active volcanic places in Europe. There is a sense of constant transformation about it all. James Hutton, one of the giants of the Enlightenment period said what geology told us is that 'we find no vestige of a beginning, no prospect of an end.' During the Ice Age glaciers swept west, broke round the old volcanic plugs and left rubble behind – and it is that rubble that gave the Old Town its shape and unique layout, with its wide high street and the narrow closes that come off it.

The topography, the shape of the town, had implications for people and buildings. Unlike England, where cities had different areas for the upper classes and the working classes, in Edinburgh the social classes lived closer together. You can visit Gladstone's Land to see a good example of a block of apartments and the way people shared space in the 17th century. Shops were on the ground floor, above them a tearoom, the second floor was for the building's owners and the floors above would house the working classes. And you never had just one ground floor or just one entrance. In that way Edinburgh is a very three-dimensional city, Victoria Street being a fascinating example of that. You have a street of shops on either side and because the ground rises so quickly you have yet more shops on the roofs of the building, which in itself creates a second street.

Going up high places and looking at the city below is what I love most.

You can go up to the highest point in the Botanic Gardens to get all those views of the Old Town skyline across the way. Or go to Calton Hill instead - I love the way the Beltane Festival has appropriated the site for their pagan celebrations in April. If you enjoy golf don't miss out on Braid Hills No. 2 course which is quite irregular and fantastic for playing. You get the whole city as a backdrop to your game. There are so many places where you can take in the views: walk up the stairs of the Scott Monument, grab a window seat at the Outsider Restaurant or dine al fresco at Pizza Express in Stockbridge.

I have great memories of going to The Waverley Bar in the 1970s, at the height of the folk music scene. I still go to the old Victorian bars: The Shore Bar, Bennets, Clark's Bar or the The Waverley are beautifully constructed. For lunch I like to go to Marina's Café, the staff are so nice and the food very good. And if I had to recommend a few unsung architectural gems I would point people to Outlook Tower or, if you fancy a swim, try one of Edinburgh's great Victorian Baths."

See The Locals' Directory on page 134 for Malcolm's top tips.
Go to www.malcolmfraser.co.uk for more on Malcolm Fraser's work.

Really want to feel at home in Edinburgh? Then look after your self-catering here:

Stay at one of Edinburgh's most prestigious addresses in **Dunstaffnage House** on Regent Terrace, minutes from Princes St. The large airy apartment sleeps up to 5 and guests have access to 12 acres of beautiful private gardens. With great value rates based on 3 people sharing, grand living can cost much less here (12 Regent Terrace, New Town, t: 0131 556 8309, Map A4).

A secret hideaway is the quaint **Royal Scots Club Mews Cottage**. Affilated to the historic Royal Scots Club on Abercromby Place, this is a unique opportunity to stay in one of the New Town's petite stone cottages. Sleeping up to 6, with access to the Club Bar and gym next door (30 Abercromby Pl, New Town, t: 0131 556 4270, Map B3).

Go the extra Royal Mile

Yes it's a castle! Ok, it's not *the* Castle but it is the closest one to Edinburgh that you can stay in. **Dundas Castle** built in 1818 is the home of Sir Jack Stewart Clark and his wife Lady Lydia. Situated 8 miles outside the city, the castle is available for exclusive hire for groups and even as a romantic getaway for two. There's over 1000 acres of secluded grounds, a private loch (of course!) and a boathouse. Long live the King! (South Queensferry, www.dundascastle.co.uk, t: 0131 319 2039)

Scots for Weather

'<u>There's no such thing as bad weather,</u>
just the wrong clothes. Get yourself
a sexy raincoat and live a little.'

Billy Connolly

comin doon in stair-rods - raining heavily
pishing doon - pissing down rain
thunder-plump - sudden thunder shower
dreich - wet and dismal
plowtery - wet, showery, rainy
smirr - a fine drizzle of rain
dreep - steady fall of light rain
haar - mist from the east coast
snell - severe weather
skirl - high pitched sound of strong wind
pirl - gentle breeze
souch - a murmur of wind
cauld - cold
cranreuch - hoar-frost
drookit - drenched, soaking wet
northern lichts - the aurora borealis
onding - a heavy continuous fall of rain
or snow,
a downpour

Gavin takes a break on top of Corstorphine Hill

INTERVIEW:
Gavin Hastings
(rugby legend)

Gavin is the record points scorer in the history of the Scottish national rugby team, and is affectionately known in the country as 'Big Gav'. These days he's in charge of a sports management and event business and enjoys exploring Edinburgh's many running routes.

I spent a few years away from Edinburgh in my 20s and returned having met a wonderful girl who is now my wife. When you meet someone you love and are ready to settle down, Edinburgh is the perfect place to do so.

The city has an outstanding reputation for education and private schools. Being able to send your children to the same school you, your father and your grandfather went to is such a privilege – there is a wonderful sense of continuity about it.

A place that's really close to my heart is Murrayfield Stadium, the home of Scottish rugby. To get behind the scenes take a stadium tour. So many people come to Edinburgh for the Six Nations and the city comes alive with crowds on the streets singing and more men in kilts than you've ever seen before. But if you can't make it to the stadium, the Murrayfield Hotel and the Roseburn Bar are good places to soak up the atmosphere of the matches. When I played for Scotland the team used to drink in Café Royal. There was such a sense of energy and excitement in those days, just the sound of our own voices was enough to raise the roof. Such a beautiful bar with its drinking booths and elegant circular counter!

These days my sport consists of golf, squash and some running. I usually run up Corstorphine Hill, where I just follow my nose never quite knowing what I am going to come across. There will be people walking their dogs, little hidden paths amongst tall trees and on top of that you get really good views of the animals in the zoo. The Queen's Park, around the Palace, and the disused railway lines are quite good running places too with plenty of people around and incredible views.

Or, if you want to venture out further afield, take the Old Union Canal and go all the way to Ratho village. The Bridge Inn Pub serves a traditional lunch and from there you might hire a barge for a group of you. I did this for my wife's birthday party once and everybody had a fantastic time!"

See The Locals' Directory on page 134 for Gavin's top tips.
To see Gavin's new team go to www.platinum-one.co.uk

Late Spring on the Meadows

NIBBLE MUNCH GNASH CHAMP CHOMP SLURP QUAFF SLURP

DEVOUR NIP NIBBLE CRUNCH GNASH

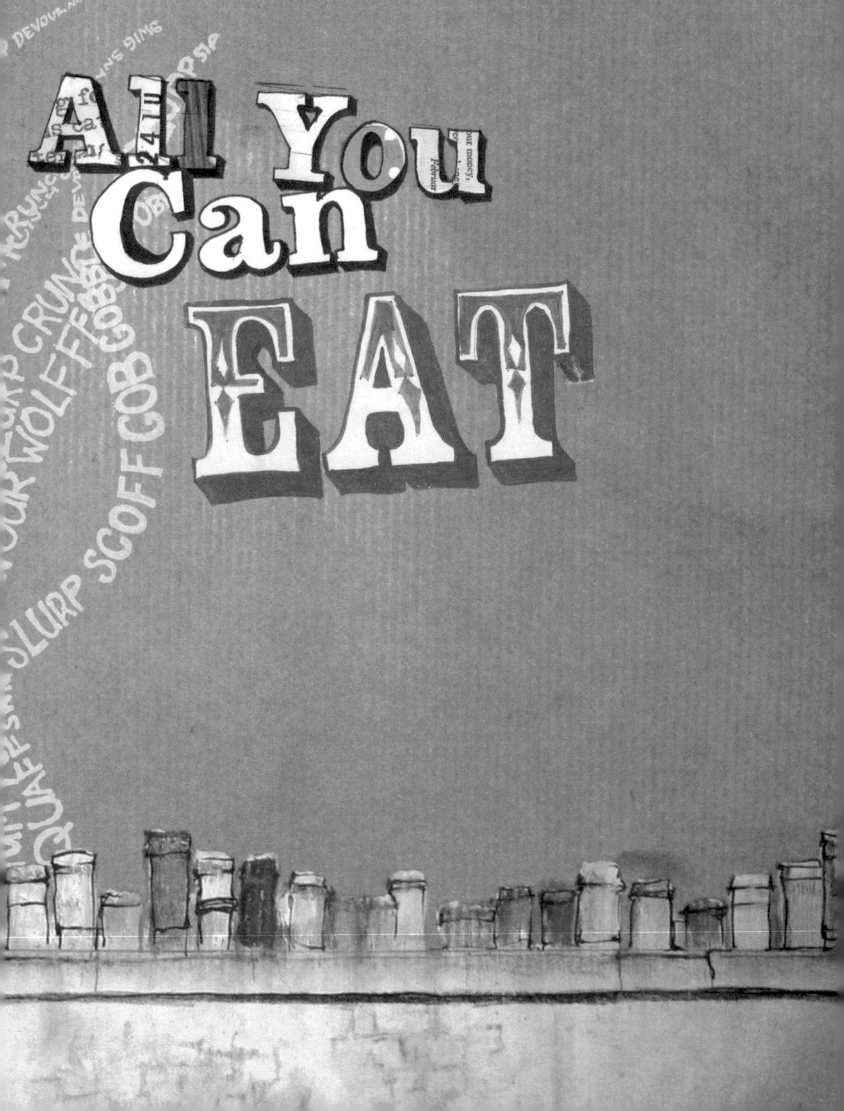
All You Can EAT
DEVOUR
SLURP SCOFF GOB
WOLF
CRUNCH
QUAFF
SIP

You know the feeling, the anticipation. You're going away and up for trying the local fare. Or maybe you live locally but can't get enough of what the city has to offer.

There's the fish, fresh off the Scottish coastline. Game, as wild as the highlands' landscape. One thousand and one Italian eateries. Old pubs with reliable grub. Sparkly fashionable restaurants and organic and eco-friendly smart cafés...

...Michelin star chefs and greasy spoons share one and the same neighbourhood. Fish and chip shops offer deep fried pizza and chips with salt 'n' sauce. Rich cakes served with cream and custard. Suddenly heart disease seems like the way to go.

Feeling hungry yet? Tuck in.
There's plenty out there.

❏Centotre ❏Quick & Plenty ❏Cloisters ❏Juice Almighty

Wake up to some good food. Morning rolls, healthy porridge, traditional Scottish or design on a plate?

The Antiquary is perfect for beating hangovers; a low lit basement pub serving full cooked breakfast straight from the kitchen of a country B&B. It comes with pots of tea, a basket of toast and a glass of juice to boot. Good eating, great value (wed-sun from 12noon, 72-78 St Stephen's St, Stockbridge, t: 0131 225 2858, Map C3).

Going to church is easy when good breakfast is the religion of choice. A converted old parsonage, **Cloisters** still has the odd pew, a fine selection of ales and fantastic cooked breakfast (every day from 12pm, except fri and sun, 26 Brougham St, Tollcross, t: 0131 221 9997, Map C5/6).

No messing. No nonsense. Breakfast in a greasy spoon café. Entering **Quick and Plenty** is like stepping into your gran's kitchen: good cups of tea and succulent bacon rolls. Cheap as chips and just as tasty (27 Leven St, Tollcross, Map C6).

Centotre's chic Italian look is popular with businessmen plotting the next take over bid on coffee and pastries. The high ceiling amplifies voices all around, creating the kind of buzz you'd expect to find in Milan (mon-sat from 8am, sun from 11am, 103 George St, New Town, t: 0131 225 1550, Map C4).

If you fancy your food dressed up then enjoy a stylish plate at **Rick's**. Blueberry pancakes, eggs benedict, waffles with fruit… And see if you can resist those bellinis from the cocktail list! (daily from 7:30am, 55a Frederick St, New Town, t: 0131 622 7800, Map C4)

Juice Almighty sells the popular Stoats Porridge – a hearty to go serving of cooked oatmeal with finger-licking toppings of fruit and nuts. This is Scottish fast food without the deadly cholesterol, guaranteed to keep you going until lunchtime (mon-sat from 7:30am, sun 10:30am, 7a Castle St, New Town, Map C4).

No time for a sit down lunch? Skip the shop stocked sandwiches for these tasty options.

Bobby's Sandwich Bar, near the courthouse, attracts well-heeled lawyers as well as lively mothers who come into town to pay their son's bail.

A good mix of sandwiches and the ultimate soup –Thai Chicken, spicy, reviving and so tasty! (4 Greyfriars Pl, Old Town, Map B5)

Don't miss **Embo's** discreet front door, where owner Mike prepares delicious Mediterranean and Eastern fillings for sandwiches. If you don't fancy bread they are happy to put all portions on a plate. The guacamole is more than delicious and the cakes divine (29 Haddington Pl, top of Leith Walk, Map A3).

Callum and his cheery staff at **Relish Deli** prepare a great cup of coffee; truly original sandwiches (try the chorizo-rich Barcelona) with the deli's ingredients and the best French bread. A true neighbourhood shop where everyone knows your name (6 Commercial St, Leith, beyond Map A1).

Paul's Original Sandwich House is worth it for the Italian Sub Hero alone. Oh. My. God. The ciabatta sub with juicy meatballs in a generous covering of mozzarella is a hungry man's dream come true (103 Hanover St, New Town, Map B4).

The lunchtime queues outside **The Baked Potato Shop** are a hint of what's to come; the tastiest spuds, good pittas and a great choice of fillings, all vegetarian. The cheery staff of this Edinburgh institution serve hungry souls until 9pm. Try the Veggie haggis and cheese! (56 Cockburn St, Old Town, Map B4)

Dining out without dressing up needn't be a let down. Try these top tips for casual comfort eating.

Avoca has the warm welcome of a local pub with the kitchen of a classy bistro. With excellent service and a menu full of tempting options, Avoca never disappoints (4-6 Dean St, Stockbridge, t: 0131 315 3311, Map D3).

Thaisanuk is a bring-your-own-bottle restaurant so small you'll be inhaling the kitchen spices the minute you walk through the door. The noodle bowls are enormous: pick from Vietnamese, Japanese, Singaporean, Malaysian, Korean or Tibetan – a great selection for around £10 (21 Argyle Pl, Marchmont, t: 0131 228 8855, Map B6).

🎵The Baked Potato Shop 🎵Thaisanuk ▪Peckhams Underground

■Monster Mash ■Rhubarb ■La Partenope

Second-generation Italians will swear by **La Partenope** as being as good as their *nona's* kitchen. The family's Naples connection really comes through the ingredients and fish plays a big part in the menu (96 Dalry Rd, Haymarket, t: 0131 347 8880, beyond Map D5).

The Blue Parrot Cantina is a wee Mexican restaurant set in a basement with an unfussy but cosy dining room. With every available inch used for tables you'll have to go outside to find the bathroom, hidden under the street! Good food, unbeatable margaritas (49 St Stephen St, Stockbridge, t: 0131 225 2941, Map C3).

There are so many reasons to go to **Monster Mash**. The staff are so upbeat and chirpy you might be fooled into thinking they've been tucking into too many of the retro sweeties at the counter. When the food arrives you realise what the fuss is all about. Old-school British grub served in generous portions (sausages and mash, steak and kidney pie, fish and chips). Add affordable prices and kitsch canteen style décor and Monster Mash is an all round winner (4a Forrest Rd, Old Town, t: 0131 225 7069, Map B5).

Go eastern at the **Mosque**. Queue through their kitchen to get your ladle of the day's dish poured on a plate and head outside to the communal tables. A rough and ready setting and, at just a few pounds this is no doubt the best value lunch in town (entrance through the archway on West Nicolson St, Old Town, t: 0131 667 1777, Map A5).

Peckhams Underground is an intimate rectangular room of stone walls and velvety seats serving Scottish and Mediterranean cooking for people with big appetites. Ask for a vegetarian or a deli delicacies platter: great to share (155-159 Bruntsfield Pl, Bruntsfield, t: 0131 228 2888, Map D7).

The Cambridge Bar is a burger lover's delight. The kitchen works with local or free range meat and vegetarians get plenty of bean-based options. Customers come first: if you're not big on bready buns they'll take them away and add more salad onto the plate (20 Young St, New Town, t: 0131 226 2120, Map C4).

Holy crêpe Batman! This food is delicious. **Le Sept** offers a slice of France in light airy high ceiling surrounds. The three course lunch is one of the best deals in town; if you have a soft spot for crêpes these are legendary. Leave room for dessert (5 Hunter Sq, Old Town, t: 0131 225 5248, Map A4).

A
TAXI

Bob casts his eye over the secret Wide Awake Club course

INTERVIEW: Bob McCulloch
(taxi driver extraordinaire)

Bob returned from a stint in West Africa and casually took on a taxi while figuring out what to do. Three decades later he's still driving passengers, guiding tourists and has published his own book, My Fare City, to celebrate some of Edinburgh's lesser known characters. Those include the incomparable Dora Noyce, who ran her house of ill repute with nothing but good manners and James Steele, the master forger who was only supplementing his age old pension with ten pence coins when the courts threw him in prison at the age of 67.

Bob believes Edinburgh is the best place to live in Britain and feels quite excited about the pace of change in the city.

Since we got the Parliament in 1999 there is a definite air of confidence about the city; there are more businesses around and the number of foreign consulates has doubled.

Scots have got this inferiority complex: we know we're good but we lack a bit of confidence. And the Parliament has given us some of that confidence back.

Sometimes you hear people complaining about the Polish coming to Edinburgh but I love the way migrants mark their presence in the city. The Italians came just after the War and that's how we got all these fish and chip shops and ice-cream places. And now the Poles are opening up all those nice delis on Leith Walk.

When it comes to eating out, I love my Italian pasta. My two favourite places are The Patio and La Partenope. I'll go there at least once a fortnight. And I am addicted to coffee; I might have six or eight cups a day. I must admit that I like my Starbucks, but Black Medicine Coffee Co. and Valvona & Crolla are two independent places that do very good coffee; Deacon's House is a good café too, set in the original workshop of Deacon Brodie. And the best fish and chip shop in Edinburgh is The Montgomery Fish Bar. A lot of taxi drivers go there for their fish suppers.

I am quite partial to a dram of whisky. Sandy Bell's is a good bar for malts and the Canny Man's has a very good selection. If you order a whisky with them it gets served in a crystal glass with a napkin, a plate of peanuts and, as the owner says, with Scottish spring water and none of that French crap.

Taxi drivers don't have a hub anymore, which is a shame. In the old days we used to run the Wide Awake Club, which was perfect for bright summer nights. We played our own golf tournament and tee-off was at half past three in the morning. It was a cheap way to do it – you just went to the golf course and made sure you finished before the staff arrived in the morning."

See The Locals' Directory on page 134 for Bob's top tips. My Fare City is published by Serendipity, London. To book Bob for a guided tour call him on 07760 282 735.

When eating is an occasion...

Scotland's food produce gets chefs jumping with joy. If you can't afford dinner, then do not miss out on the lunch offers – you can be eating food fit for the Gods for heavenly prices. Booking is essential.

The Outsider is one of the best places in town. Beautiful candle-lit décor, stunning views of the Castle and an exciting menu of uncomplicated and made-to-share fusion food. Great steak too (15-16 George IV Bridge, Old Town, t: 0131 226 313, Map B5).

A Room in the Town offers top Scottish cuisine in a relaxed and friendly setting that makes groups feel at home. This is a popular neighbourhood restaurant, made all the more affordable with a BYOB option (18 Howe St, New Town, t: 0131 225 8204, Map C3).

If you can't make it to Paris book a table at **Le Café Saint Honoré** instead. A wonderful winter's cocoon, Le Café Saint Honoré is the haunt of choice for Edinburgh's many lawyers and amorous couples looking for some *je ne sais quoi*. A traditional atmosphere with impeccable standards of service (34 North West Thistle St Lane, New Town, t: 0131 226 2211, Map C4).

Rhubarb at Prestonfield may only be a five minute taxi ride from the city centre but a visit to the 17th century mansion will feel like a longer voyage into baronial decadence. This is an A-list place, praised by hip hop legends and Hollywood actresses alike, and the closest you will get to Highland grandeur without leaving Edinburgh. It comes with its own helipad (Prestonfield, Prestonfield Road, t: 0131 225 1333, 2 miles from city centre).

Creelers serves up some of Scotland's finest seafood. Twinned with a sister restaurant by the same name on the Isle of Arran, its owners Tim and Fran James bring their West Coast fishing roots and years of expertise to the table. Keep an eye out for Tim's catch at the Farmer's Market (3 Hunter Sq, Old Town, t: 0131 220 4447, Map A4).

🔲Le Café St Honoré 🔲The Outsider 🔲Patisserie Florentin 🔲Susie's Wholefood Diner

And for those who care for their vegetables...

The people behind **Susie's Wholefood Diner** are really committed to cooking incredible vegetarian food in filling combinations at low prices, in a no-frills, wooden canteen atmosphere. This place will make meat-eaters think twice (51-53 West Nicolson St, Southside, t: 0131 667 8729, Map A5).

David Bann's is the crème de la crème of vegetarian eating in the city. It's a grown-up establishment, with imaginative cooking well beyond predictable risottos and goat's cheese tartines (56-58 St Mary's St, Old Town, t: 0131 5565888, Map A4).

It's late. I mean really late. There is nothing open except...

Perfect as a party pit stop, **Negoçiants** is an ideal spot to add some much needed nourishment to your night out before hitting the clubs. Open till 3 for drinks and serving straight forward fuel food up to 2am, this bustling bistro allows you to continue partying post-pub and pre-club without breaking your stride (45-47 Lothian St, Old Town, t: 0131 225 6313, Map B5).

Bar Roma keeps its doors open until 1am on Fridays and Saturdays. There are over 30 pasta dishes on the menu - a late table here can turn even the worst night around (39a Queensferry St, West End, t: 0131 226 2977, Map D4).

(see also take-aways on page 55)

Take a break from Edinburgh's hills and rest your tired legs with a cup of coffee...

Get inspired in **Patisserie Florentin**. Its tables are not unknown to local writers and the French cakes, salads and pastas should keep your taste buds happy. Go through the back for some genteel tearoom atmosphere (5 North West Circus Pl, Stockbridge, Map C3).

INTERVIEW: David Ramsden

(restaurateur)

David learned his trade at Le Caprice in London. He returned to Scotland and ran Fitzhenry's and his own Rogue, both Michelin starred on his watch. He currently manages The Outsider restaurant.

66 When it comes to eating out I don't do "bottom of the market". I would say that for top eating right now it has got to be The Kitchin, Tom Kitchin's restaurant. Tom has managed to grasp the zeitgeist in every way: his place has good atmosphere, the right amount of contemporary art, and his food is really good. Fresh Scottish produce handled superbly!

The middle end of the market is not where I usually dine but there's a place I really recommend and have been going to for the last 25 years, The Himalaya in Bruntsfield. It is ruthlessly dependable and has the best curries in town. And The Outsider, of course. Not just because it is where I work but because it is good value, nice food, got a bit of a buzz and has pretty girls and boys around. For café food I go to Spoon - I love the people behind this one. Richie Alexander was my first chef at the Rogue and that man has got magic hands – he opened the café to put more soul into his food and get away from the pressure of fine dining.

If you want to find some wild foods, Blackford Hill is a great place to pick up berries and wild garlic. And for buying fresh Scottish produce the only spot to go to is the Farmer's Market on a Saturday. That stuff should really be supported and it is a great place to meet other people and chat to the producers.

Any free time I have is spent with my two big dogs, who demand a lot of attention and exercise – Arthur's Seat and Blackford Hill are ideal. Sometimes I just stand up there and spin for the craic of it – you've got unbeatable panoramic views. On a clear day you can see Glasgow, England, the mountains, everything..."

See The Locals' Directory on page 135 for David's top tips.
The Outsider, 15-16 George IV Bridge, t: 0131 226 3131, Map B5.

David and his dog reach the summit of Blackford Hill

♩The Portrait Gallery ♫The Fruitmarket Gallery Café ♬Balmoral Hotel

Black Medicine Coffee Co. is the students' hangout of choice, with dark moody interiors and rustic custom-made wooden tables and seats. Lots of reading choices, plenty of smoothies, tasty bagels and paninis (2 Nicolson St, Old Town, Map A5).

An elegant Milanese café, **Sprio** serves the best (and most garlicky) bruschettas in Edinburgh to the sound of Italian radio (37 St Stephen St, Stockbridge, Map C3).

Beanscene is *the* late night café in Edinburgh, showcasing live music. BYOB means more than just bring your own band - you can bring your own booze too! (99 Nicolson St, Southside; more branches in Leith, Haymarket and Holyrood, until 11pm, Map A5, beyond Map A1, beyond Map D5 and Map A4 respectively)

...fancy some cake with your coffee?

The Fruitmarket Gallery Café is said to have the best brownies in Edinburgh and the rhubarb tart is a shrine to all things sweet (45 Market St, Old Town, Map B4).

Go grand with afternoon tea at the five-star **Balmoral Hotel**. Finger sandwiches, scones, tea and a mouth-watering selection of cakes. Get served in The Bolinger Bar at Palm Court for the full royal experience, accompanied by a harpist (1 Princes St, New Town, 2:30-5:30pm, Map B4).

Falko Konditormeister's respect for traditional methods and ingredients is only matched by the lightness of his creations. Trying one of Falko's cakes is essential for anyone who takes their confectionery seriously, but be warned seating is limited to two tables (7 Bruntsfield Pl, Bruntsfield, closes sun, Map C6; also at The Farmer's Market on Castle Terrace, sat only till 2pm, Map C5).

The Queen Street Café at the Portrait Gallery sells home-baked cakes in a grand neo-gothic setting, and the café is framed by the overwhelming stained glass windows (1 Queen St, New Town, Map B3). You can't go wrong with any of the national galleries; take the free bus to the Modern Art and Dean Gallery for a complete cake and art tour of the city.

And last but not the least, check out the cakes at **Manna House**. Mike and Anna fall under the spell of these sweet treats on the next page.

INTERVIEW:
Anna & Mike Christopherson

(parents & publicans)

Anna and Mike visited Edinburgh for a week and fell for the city instantly. They went back home to Stockholm, packed their car and arrived in Leith without really knowing much about the place. Their search for a friendly local led them to convert a shabby old pub on Leith Walk into a cosy living room-like bar called Boda, welcoming old regulars and new visitors alike. The concept caught on and Sofi's Bar near the Shore soon followed, as did Victoria just up the road from Boda.

❝ We're delighted the bars are so popular. When we first looked at Boda we were told the room in the back was called the 'fighting room' and rumour was that someone had been murdered there! Only then did we get an idea of what a job we had on our hands. Now though, with so many young people moving to Leith, we get a good mixed crowd. You can be drinking here with people from all over the world and in Victoria's our international beer menu reflects this.

Edinburgh is great like that: international but also small enough that you can bump into people you know on the street. If we had been brought up in Edinburgh and knew the city better we probably wouldn't have thought of investing in Leith Walk. But we're really happy we did. It's a friendly part of town and the people are really genuine.

When it comes to eating out one of our absolute favourite places to eat is Dusit, the Thai Restaurant on Thistle Street. It has the best Thai food in the city and the people are so lovely. It's on a bit of a hidden street so make sure you don't miss it. We also like going to Harvey Nicks Fourth Floor Restaurant, they have the

Anna, Mike and their children – Manna House

best fries in the whole of Edinburgh! Not a lot of people know this, but their restaurant is really family friendly, they're great with kids. Sometimes when we want to feel grown up we go to Tigerlily – Anna recognises every single piece of their décor from old design magazines. We live on the top of Leith Walk and go to Manna House on Easter Road for cakes – they look like pieces of art! Mike ventures into The Union of Communication Workers every now and then for a pint. It's a really old social club for postal workers. The landlady is a real character and there's a great beer garden outside, so you can take your dog along with you.

Looking for furniture in need of some TLC is another one of our hobbies. We go to a lot of auctions and trek along the shops in Bruntsfield and Causewayside. Furniture from the 1950s and 1960s is the best for our bars, it was made better then so it's strong and resistant. We mix it with some modern things – Designshop has a good selection of contemporary designs."

See the Locals' Directory on page 135 for Anna and Mike's top tips.
Boda (229 Leith Walk, beyond Map A2), Sofi's (65 Henderson St, Leith, beyond Map A1), Victoria (265, Leith Walk, beyond Map A2), Pearce's Bar (25 Elm Row, top of Leith Walk, Map A3).

Whether it's the last stop home on the way back from the pub or the saving grace in a stressful day, these are Edinburgh's fast food favourites.

L'Alba d'Oro is about the finer chips in life: the vast wine cellar attracts a loyal clientele, and even the simplest of affairs is done with flair – every week there is a special guest fish whether luxurious or from far flung shores (7 Henderson Row, New Town, closes 11pm all week, t: 0131 557 2580, Map C2).

If you haven't experienced enough dancing by the time you go for your take-away then try **Piccante** on a Friday or Saturday, when this bright outfit crams a resident DJ next to the chip fryer! (19 Broughton St, New Town, closes 3am fri-sat, 2am rest of the week, t: 0131 478 7884, Map A3)

Home to one of the best cups of coffee, **Made In Italy** is also a welcome alternative to the chippy for Grassmarket revellers. Top calzone, stromboli and pizza – among the best in town (42 Grassmarket, Old Town, closes at 11pm mon-thurs, 2am fri-sat, 9:30pm sun, t: 0131 622 7328, Map B5).

Mediterranean Gate has a dizzying list of Middle Eastern options and is the number one stop for Edinburgh's falafel fanatics. Open 'til the early hours, one post-pub visit and you'll never have chips on the way home again (48 George IV Bridge, Old Town, closes at 3am fri-sat, 9.30pm rest of the week, t: 0131 220 3696, Map B5).

Malone's Bakeries is a hungry insomniac's dream. All types of rolls and bran scones are served fresh off the oven of this wholesaler until 4am on Saturdays and 9am on Sundays (113-115 Slateford Rd, off Dalry Rd, 2.5 miles from city centre, t: 0131 337 7621).

Go shopping and stock your pantry with some of these amazing foods...

For meat, head to **George Bower's**, a proper butcher's butcher with dead animals hanging on the window, a reliable selection of game and the most aromatic haggis in the city (75 Raeburn Pl, Stockbridge, Map D3).

Eddie's Seafood Market George Bower's Valvona & Crolla

Eddie's Seafood Market supplies many of the city's restaurants. Expect an inch of seawater on the floor (you'll be walking on raised plastic platforms) and buckets of whole fish scattered throughout the place (75 Roseneath St, Marchmont, Map B6).

Valvona & Crolla is often judged as the best deli in the UK, and has been trading for over 75 years. Buy some Italian treasures (including fine wines) or try them on a plate – the backroom restaurant serves grandmother's cooking 'til 3pm and stays open until 6pm for coffee and cakes (19 Elm Row, top of Leith Walk, Map A3).

Sample Scotland's finest at **The Farmer's Market**. Farmers, fishmongers, bakers, vegetable growers and jam-makers all gather here to sell their stuff and cook a bit on the side. Grab an ostrich burger or a bucket of seafood (Castle Terrace, Old Town, Map C5).

Cheese lovers should run to **Ian Mellis** stores. Artisan cheeses from the four corners of Scotland and other foreign varieties, all explained through clever 'cheese for dummies' labels (30a Victoria St, Old Town, 205 Bruntsfield Pl, Bruntsfield, 6 Bakers Pl, Stockbridge, Map B5, D7, D3 respectively).

The Sicilian Pastry Shop is a Leith institution. Open since 1979, the small shopfront disguises an extensive bakery, famous for celebration cakes. If it's not your birthday don't worry, there's also a fab selection of colourful Italian cakes, fruit tarts and delicious doughnuts (14-16 Albert St, off Leith Walk, beyond Map A2).

INTERVIEW:
Mary Contini

(chef, deli owner, author)

❝ Both mine and my husband's grandfathers came from the same tiny Italian village in the Abruzzi Mountains in the 1920s as young lads. And the story goes they walked all the way to Scotland! Alfonso and Cesidio eventually opened ice-cream shops and prospered. Alfonso Crolla became the leader of the community and his business, Valvona & Crolla, was the first port of call for the chain of Italian migrants who arrived in Edinburgh throughout the 20th century.

It fills me with pride to think of the wealth of talent that originates from those remote villages. People assume Italians stick to the restaurant business, but as a matter of fact they have been shaping the life of this city through law, architecture, arts and medicine. I feel huge admiration every time I walk into The Royal College of Surgeons and look at the portrait of Professor Arnold Maran. He symbolises all of those who've become part of the Scottish establishment, becoming one of the top ear, nose and throat surgeons in the world. There are so many others. Take the sculptor Eduardo Paolozzi – who went to school in Leith with my mother-in-law, Alfonso's daughter. He was eventually knighted for services to art.

For anyone wanting to research their family history I recommend a visit to The Edinburgh Room at The National Library – you can browse through old maps and phonebooks, find out where your relatives used to live, and uncover family heritage. I love visiting the Dean Gallery to contemplate Eduardo Paolozzi's studio. This exhibition of the artist's work provides clues to Italian immigration into Scotland. The Church of Our Lady of Loretto is another of my favourite places, it offers quite a contrast to Edinburgh's Calvinistic and austere churches.

Nowadays I live near the east coast of Edinburgh where my grandfather Cesidio settled. There is so much to discover out there: ancient fishing villages, deserted beaches and lovely walks. I love Inveresk Village with its stunning and very individual houses, built in the 16th and 17th centuries by merchants and bankers who wanted to escape the smog of the city. Inveresk Gardens are well worth a visit and many of the private gardens have open days that should not be missed – some of the resident families might even offer you tea and cakes!❞

Valvona & Crolla (19 Elm Row, top of Leith Walk, Map A3)
See The Locals' Directory on page 135 for Mary's top tips.

Mary at the altar in the Church of Our Lady of Loretto

Martin Wishart's Cullen Skink
(haddock, leek & potato soup)
serves 4 – 6

- 50g unsalted butter
- 250g white leeks
- 1 small sized Yukon gold potato
- 1 small sized onion
- 250ml chicken stock

- 150ml double cream
- 250ml boiling water
- 200ml milk
- 400g Finnan haddock
  (smoked haddock)

Wash the leeks and discard any dark green. Finely slice the onion and leeks and place aside. Pour the cream, chicken stock and water into a large saucepan and bring to the boil. Melt the butter in a heavy based saucepan and add the leeks and onions. Gently sauté without colouring for 5-8 minutes. Add the boiling liquid and cook for 5 minutes. Peel and finely slice the potato and add to the soup. Boil for a further 10 minutes and remove from the heat. Pour the soup into a liquidiser and blend for 5 minutes, so the soup becomes silky in texture. Poach the smoked haddock in milk for 4-5 minutes and remove. Carefully flake the smoked haddock using your fingers, into 4 soup bowls. Warm the soup and pour over the haddock. Sprinkle with chopped chives and serve.

Restaurant Martin Wishart (54 Shore, Leith, beyond Map A1)
Booking essential, t: 0131 553 3557, open tue-sat.

1 Recipe,,,

Trainspotting (1996, Danny Boyle)

The film that brought Irvine Welsh's dark amoral humour to the masses defined a generation. Set in Edinburgh (but filmed mostly in Glasgow), the seedy underbelly of heroin addiction forms the backdrop to the adventures of a group of addicts and their attempts to quit the drug. Fast-paced, graphic and scathing, the film was lauded by critics around the world and made broad Scots tongue finally understood in Hollywood.

Festival (2005, Annie Griffin)

Annie Griffin perfectly captures the madness of Edinburgh in August and the many facets of the Fringe Festival. Performers' hopes, dreams and egos – it's all there. The story follows the build up to a major comedy award (based on the Perrier Award) while interweaving the subplots of various festival characters with trademark dark and cynical humour.

The Prime of Miss Jean Brodie by Muriel Spark.

Miss Brodie is an eccentric and controversial teacher who takes a group of private school girls under her tutelage – they are to be the 'crème de la crème'. But her contradictory morals and independent spirit land her in trouble, and betrayal develops within her own circle. Morningside ladies and Calvinist values abound in one of the most powerful Scottish works of the 20th century.

Hide & Seek by Ian Rankin

Rankin's popular detective Rebus probes the unexplained death of a junkie, an investigation that takes him through the high and low life of the city – from the exclusive clubs frequented by politicians to the dark underworld that lies beneath Edinburgh's picture-perfect setting. Rankin pays homage to Robert Louis Stevenson's Dr Jekyll and Mr Hyde and fleshes out the classic dualities of Edinburgh, with Rebus exploring the darker side of his own character.

,2 Films, 2 Books

'[Dr Johnson] *always said that he was not come to Scotland to see fine places, of which there were enough in England; but wild objects – mountains, waterfalls, peculiar manners; in short, things which he had not seen before.*'

James Boswell, The Journal of a Tour to the Hebrides
with Samuel Johnson LLD (1786)

If you can't take the trip out to the Hebrides, just like Boswell and his good friend Johnson did, do not worry. Walking through Edinburgh is like stepping inside the pages of a dramatic pop-up book, with imposing rock faces on Arthur's Seat, tranquil glens and waterfalls nestled amongst the Pentland Hills, and tree-lined meandering paths along the flowing streams of the Water of Leith. When in Scotland do as the Scots: embrace the elements and go for a walk.

Water of Leith

The walk from Stockbridge to the Modern Art Galleries, near Roseburn, is one of the city's most romantic landscapes with dramatic weirs, fantastic stone bridges, disused nineteenth century flour mills and some beautiful wildlife – you might even spot an otter or an elegant heron along the way.

Enter the Water of Leith from Stockbridge, turn into Saunders Street and follow the water upstream. Carry on for 1¼ miles through Dean Village until you reach the signposted steps on the right hand side that take you up to the galleries. Catch the work of Henry Moore and don't miss out on the sculptured garden. You might want to round it off with one of the café's delicious cakes. There is a free bus back to the city centre for those wishing to rest their feet.

Hermitage of Braid and Blackford Hill

On the southern end of the city, Hermitage of Braid and Blackford Hill are the places to explore if you find yourself in Marchmont or Bruntsfield. Like the Mad Hatter's tea party, this route is an ever-changing feast of unexpected surprises; a lush green glen, a lively burn* shaded by trees, a wildflower meadow, paths bordered by raspberries, bluebells and wild roses – all this at the foot of an open summit with stunning views of the city and sea. Walk takes between 45 and 90 minutes.

Your walk starts by taking the entrance into the Hermitage of Braid on the bottom of Braid Road, 2 minutes from the main thoroughfare of Morningside. You'll find yourself naturally walking along the right bank of the river, which takes you on well defined circular loop of Hermitage of Braid, past the visitor centre (where you can pick up a route map) and on through the woodlands. You will cross a significant wooden bridge at which point the path begins its ascent upwards. Don't miss out on the chance to go even higher to the top of Blackford Hill. From an open grassy area on the right of the path there is an obvious short sharp ascent that takes you up to a radio aerial mast. The summit is visible to your left. Having reached the top, descend down a zigzag path (looking to the city centre, the path is to the left of the Royal Observatory building) which will lead you down to the base of the hill. Keeping the hill on your left continue to walk until you come upon the open grassy area, where you can resume the circular loop of Hermitage of Braid back to the beginning.

*scots for wee river.

Arthur's Seat into Duddingston Village

Hike up Edinburgh's most impressive geological landmark and recuperate in the city's oldest and cosiest of pubs, The Sheep Heid Inn. Walk takes approximately 1 hour.

Starting from the car park to the side of Palace of Holyroodhouse, the route to the top is almost a direct assault on Edinburgh's miniature mountain, Arthur's Seat. Cross the road and head along the path away from the city. Keep the Crags (rock cliffs) to your right and head towards the valley, then take the path up Arthur's left shoulder. The path is well trodden to the top, but becomes steeper and rockier as you go. Take care – especially in the wind and rain. It won't be easy to give up those 360 degree views of Edinburgh once you reach the top. Take your time. When you're ready make your way down by taking the wide grassy paths to the east, with the main road (Queen's Drive) by the lochin* in clear view. Once you get to the road take a right then carry straight on, stopping just before the iron railings that border the pavement – this is where you turn left to take the steps down to Duddingston Village. At the bottom of the steps make a sharp left and follow the walled path – The Sheep Heid Inn's cosy setting will be in sight. With batteries recharged and ready to return, walk back into town via the pavement that leads out of the village (30 minutes approximately; alternatively take bus 4 or 44, bus stop is 10 minutes away from the village).

Pentland Hills

For a slice of wilderness right on the doorstep of the city head to the Pentland Hills. With over 100km of paths and 10,000 hectares of countryside this is an incredible landscape to explore, and everyone – from walkers, to horse riders and cyclists – flocks here for a taste of remoteness. Both Flotterstone Village and Harlaw are good places to start from, their visitor centres act as gateways to the hills and can provide you with maps for orientation. To find out more go to www.pentlandhills.org or phone 0870 608 2608 for bus times.

*lochin - a small Scottish land locked lake.

Heron fishing on the water of Leith

View of Arthur's Seat from Blackford Hill

INTERVIEW:
Nick Thorpe
(author)

Nick made Edinburgh his home in the mid-1990s. A decade later, still feeling he was only floating on the surface of Scotland, he went boat-hitching through the nation's canals, lochs, islands and coastal waters – on what he called a nautical sabbatical. Pondering the meaning of life for 2500 miles didn't bring many clear-cut answers, but it taught him to enjoy the questions…

❝ Being near water is really important to me. The old Union Canal is like a parallel universe in itself. One minute you're in a busy street, then suddenly you turn a corner and find yourself in this long, peaceful backwater. On Sunday afternoons you can rent a boat from a little white hut off Ashley Terrace, run by the friendly eccentrics at Edinburgh Canal Society.

You can get the same unexpected peace in the city centre just by nipping down one of those little closes off the Royal Mile. When I worked for The Scotsman newspaper I used to dodge into one with my lunch to escape the crowds. All of a sudden you'd be in a little walled garden, with birds singing. Wonderful.

As a place to write, I like Starbucks in Waterstone's bookshop at the West End, in front of that huge window that looks out onto the castle. Failing that, I might go to Caffé Lucano, or the National Library of Scotland if I really need to knuckle down. If you're there, check out the John Murray Archive with its vast number of papers from 19th century writers. You can find yourself looking at the original letter Charles Darwin sent to his publisher with the draft of The Origin of Species - or the correspondence of Lord Byron and David Livingstone. The Socrates Café is a great place to go to on a winter's Sunday – a people's philosophy club where you can discuss anything from fundamentalism to the meaning of independence.

I like pubs that are vaguely nautical. The Old Chain Pier used to be a ticket booth for old steamers, and the back windows look straight onto the sea. After a bowl of their great lamb stew, I like to wander down to Newhaven harbour for one of my favourite views: the lighthouse silhouetted against a purple sunset, preferably at low tide, the boats all lying wistful-looking on their sides. Very romantic."

See The Locals' Directory on page 135 for Nick's top tips.

Nick's favourite view

Being near water is really
important...
union ca...
universe...
you;.re...
then sudde...
and find...
long, be...
You can...
peace in...
by nippi...
closes do...
When I wo...
I used to...
lunch to...
of a sudd...
walled...
Wonderful.

Nick Thorpe's book, Adrift in Caledonia, Boat-hitching for
the Unenlightened is published by Abacus, £7.99.
Details: www.nickthorpe.co.uk

Cold Comforts

It's freezing outside... what do you do?

On a cold winter's day, few things feel better than jumping into **Sheraton's One Spa outdoor heated pool**. And if it snows that's your lucky day – watch the flakes cover the city while you're surrounded by steam and hot bubbling water (8 Conference Sq, off Lothian Rd, £65 Mon-Fri, weekend access restricted to those who book treatments, t: 0131 221 7777, Map C5).

The King's Wark is a gigantic bear-hug of a pub. The huge fireplace is the perfect antidote to wind-battered Leith and the food substantial enough to keep you hibernating all the way through to spring (36 Shore, Leith, beyond Map A1).

Join the exclusive **The Scotch Malt Whisky Society**, or alternatively head there on a Thursday night, when the restaurant opens to the public. You need to book a table for dinner to get a chance to taste the golden malts that come from over 100 distilleries in Scotland. The Society has some rare treats, and the widest selection of single cask, cask strength malts anywhere in the world (28 Queen St, New Town, to book t: 0131 220 2044, Map C3).

Pop into the **Scottish Storytelling Centre**, right on the Royal Mile and listen to some live oral storytelling and traditional folktales (**43-45 High St, Map A4**). Whether you choose to attend one of their many events or not, make sure to tuck into some of the café's delicious soup while you're there. Of course we can't mention comfort food without recommending haggis, neeps 'n' tatties (that's turnip and potatoes), the gastronomic equivalent of a lambswool blanket. **Whiski** on the Royal Mile serves up a hearty helping (**119, High St, Map A4**). Comfort on a plate comes with traditional British cooking in **Monster Mash**, a retro canteen-style setup (**4a, Forrest Rd, Map B5**).

December is **Christmas fair** time. Go ice-skating in Princes Street Gardens and soak up the spirit of the season with a mug of mulled wine (the German market stalls sell apple strudel that is not to be missed either, Map B4). You can take your winter sports further and head to **Midlothian Snowsports Centre** at Hillend. Grab a number 4 bus from the garden side of Princes Street which will take you to the foot of the slopes. It's open all year round except for a couple of weeks in June (**To book lessons call in advance, t: 0131 445 4433**).

Embrace the elements, go for a **morning walk**, and finish with a hearty pub meal. You can buy good water and windproof clothes in Tiso's (**123 Rose St or 41 Commercial St, Map C4**) and try one of the walks on page 67 – the trek up Arthur's Seat and down into the old village of Duddingston is a good option. If walking's not your thing, then head to **Dance Base** for a drop-in class and get your feet moving. There are nearly 50 options on offer, covering a broad range of styles: Scottish dances, tap dancing, jazz, breakdance & hip hop, ballroom and world dances (**14-16 Grassmarket, t: 0131 225 5525, Map B5**). If you fancy a well-earned massage after all that exercise call Lou at **Tonic Health** on t: 0131 554 6161.

Christmas Fair Carousel

BE MERRY

just the one?

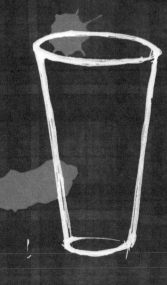

A cityscape of nooks and crannies, closes and wynds lends itself to a rabbit warren network of hidden away pubs and hostelries, watering holes for the early risers and late nighters. Wish-you-were-in-London cocktail bars jostle cheek and jowl with dingy dimly lit traditional pubs. A safe haven from the ever changeable weather, the pub in all its shapes and sizes continues to be the heartbeat of the city's social scene. To enjoy Edinburgh from the inside out pull up a stool. Order a quiet pint, try decadent cocktails, plan big nights out, bask in long summer evenings or huddle in a cosy retreat.

"Fancy a pint? Ah go on, just the one. I know this great place…"

♪Dragonfly ♬Kay's Bar ♩Victorias ♭Tigerlily

Pubs have either a drinking license until 1am or during festival time, an extended license until 3 in the morning. Opening hours can be anything between 12 noon and 6pm, depending on the establishment. As a rule of thumb expect last call at 11.45 during the week or 12.45 on weekends, unless it's mentioned otherwise.

When you want to step right into the middle of a jumping night out walk through these doors, with party shoes on...

Top tunes and a cocktail menu longer than the bar that serves it, **Tonic** is a compact party pressure cooker. Louder than most and dressed up to the nines, its infectious energy will kickstart the most subdued nights out (34a North Castle St, New Town, Map C4).

The jewel in the crown of Edinburgh's style scene has raised the bar across the board. With an interior straight off the pages of Wallpaper Magazine and a crowd dressed to match, **Tigerlily** is the place to go for designer drinks. Make sure to explore all the different spaces; smokers are catered for, outdoor style, in the bar's smoking room. If you've got your dancing shoes on then head downstairs to Lulu (125 George St, New Town, Map C4).

The Outhouse is a wee laid back hideaway attracting all kinds of drinkers. The beer garden space is larger than the pub itself and Sunday summer barbeques make the most of this, with resident DJs every week. Year round the combination of the anything-goes-crowd and funky playlist can find you dancing in even the smallest patches of floor space (12a Broughton St Lane, New Town, Map A3).

Welcome to **Villager,** a chilled cocktail hangout with a tasty but unfussy food menu. Half of Villager is for diners, which only heightens the atmosphere in the limited space in front of the bar, where cool-for-school staff serve up the greatest hits from an extensive drinks list. Look out for the 80s retro ghetto blasters (49-50 George IV Bridge, Old Town, Map B5).

Play.

Jude runs Grid Iron Theatre Company.
Check www.gridiron.org.uk to find out about their latest productions.

Jude in the Barony Bar

INTERVIEW:
Jude Doherty
(theatre producer)

Jude produces theatre in unusual places, and places are something she cares and is stubborn about. Jude famously got the Department of Transport to temporarily change the law on airside borders at Edinburgh Airport for two hours every day in order to stage the award-winning play Roam. And a few years back she chased the City Council until they let her into an abandoned underground building, now one of the most successful festival venues, Underbelly. When Grid Iron scout for locations for their plays, they make sure those locations come with very decent pubs nearby, wherever they are in the world. This is the sort of woman you should listen to if you care about your pints.

" "

Every time we do a show abroad I think I could move there but then I come back to this city and fall in love with it all over again. Years ago I saw the comedian Spike Milligan being interviewed on TV for the Edinburgh Show and he said this was the most exciting place to be. I knew then I had to live here.

The Broughton area is my spiritual home in Edinburgh, and I need to be within shooting distance of the Barony Bar. You will recognize the locals easily – they're the people standing up or sitting on the bar stools by the entrance. And the Barony is great to go to as a solo girl without being intimidated; the crowd there are so relaxed. But if you are on a date I would head to Teuchters instead. It can be quiet enough to feel like an intimate space but busy enough that you won't find yourself in those silent awkward moments. Sometimes I quite fancy more of a spit-and-sawdust pub like The Oxford Bar.

For a dose of normality the Thistle Street Bar is great. When winter arrives you just want places that offer that comforting feeling, the King's Wark is perfect for that, with the big fire and subdued lighting. Summer days should be celebrated with a visit to The Shore Bar – you can bring your drink outside, sit on the edge of the wharf and dangle your feet over the water."

See The Locals' Directory on page 136 for Jude's top tips.

The sexy sister pub to Villager, **Dragonfly** is the reward for going through the Grassmarket and not stopping at any of the other pubs on the way. Funky and flash in equal measure, art school chic and streetwear savvy combine to give a fun and flirty feel that complements the retro furniture (52 West Port, just off The Grassmarket, Old Town, Map C5).

Cosy, casual and created for comfort, the following choices are the city's dress down drinking dens...

A pub's pub. There is not one outstanding feature that makes the **Thistle Street Bar** great. Cosy fireplace, friendly staff, limited space and just the right mix of regulars and visitors all combine to make this unassuming watering hole one of the best bars in Edinburgh (39 Thistle St, New Town, Map C4).

At first glance from the street, **Kay's Bar** looks like it was plucked from a village in the Outer Hebrides and dropped in the middle of the New Town. Its red walls and wee stools give the impression of a friendly living room while the staff and neighbourhood regulars make you feel welcome with traditional ales and an extensive whisky list. A home for rugby fans, the living room feel is more house party on international rugby days (39 Jamaica St, New Town, Map C3).

Burlington Bertie's can be found down a side street from the King's Theatre. Old men and a younger scruffy crowd drink side by side and the legendary jukebox makes for a welcoming atmosphere. Perfect for a pre, during and post theatre pint (11-13 Tarvit St, Tollcross, Map C6).

The greatest additions to the Edinburgh drinking scene are the Swedish drinking dens, **Bar Boda, Sofi's and Victoria**. Boda was the first pub you could drink in on Leith Walk without fear of being beaten up for having anything less or more than a pint and a nip. They have a great selection of wine and drinks, art on the walls and tasty bar snacks served in homely-fashion. Keep an eye out for moose sausage and a delicious selection of Swedish confectionery. Sofi's in Leith continues the trend and Victoria Bar is Boda's best next door neighbour (Bar Boda, 229 Leith Walk, beyond Map A1. Sofi's, 65 Henderson St, Leith, beyond Map B1. Victoria, 265 Leith Walk, beyond Map A1).

Sometimes the most enjoyable nights out are in the company of just one other person, so whether you're catching up or making out here's where to head...

The Waverley is the stuff of legend, a beautiful Victorian bar and probably the only one where there's more space behind the counter than in front of it. The owner is known but never referred to as The Captain; his unwritten rules include no swearing or using mobile phones. In return customers are graced with free crisps, the choice of just 3 different beers on tap and a shabby interior covered in posters from festivals gone by (3-5 St Mary's St, Old Town, Map A4).

The black marble bar in **Brass Monkey** is one of the nicest in the city to sit at. With two main seating areas and a screening room space, this small pub can fill up quickly, so a one-on-one drink at the bar is often the best option. When you do come back with a group pre-book the screening room and pick from the classic movies on offer (14 Drummond St, Old Town, to book t: 0131 556 1961 Map A5).

The basic appearance of **Black Bo's** belies its unique charm. A hideout for journalists from The Scotsman and The List Magazine, the cosy space is also shared by lucky visitors from the hostel across the road. The mix of global and local makes this wee pub a perfect spot to avoid the tourist crowds (57-61 Blackfriars St, off the Royal Mile, Old Town, Map A4).

For anyone tired of trekking up and down the Royal Mile, keep an eye out for an escape route at James Court. Just down the vennel lies **The Jolly Judge.** Low beamed ceilings (many covered in international banknotes) and a cosy fireplace welcome the weary. The only sounds you'll hear will be the chatter of fellow drinkers. If a quiet pint is in order, here's where it's at (7 James Court Lawnmarket, off the top of the Royal Mile, Old Town, Map B4).

Fiona at home in Black Bo's

INTERVIEW:
Fiona Donegan
(student)

Fiona came over from Dublin only intending to spend a few weeks in Edinburgh. But then the festival started and she couldn't bring herself to leave. Bitten by the bug, she decided to join in the fun and enrolled in the Festivals and Events course at Napier University.

One of the things I love about Edinburgh is that you keep discovering new places, every neighbourhood has its own hideaway pubs and shops that you might never come across. Not only do these day-to-day discoveries make the city exciting, there's also a huge number of events happening. People are constantly encouraged to interact with the city and its landscape whether through communal bonfires on Guy Fawkes night or by taking part in something as large as the festival.

With so many universities in Edinburgh, the entire city has a student feel to it. There are plenty of student bars but I prefer to go to places where the crowd is more mixed and everyone is welcome. My favourite spot for a drink is Black Bo's. The pub attracts all types: journalists working nearby, backpackers staying at the hostel across the way and people who work in the restaurant trade. It's also really popular with musicians, I often see The Fence Collective in there and The Fratelli's usually pop in, if they're in town. The great thing about Bo's though is that everyone is treated the same, there's no airs and graces at the bar. One regular describes it as one big happy family - The Munsters!

As a treat I like to take people to Wildfire on Rose Street. It serves the best steaks in Edinburgh! With only nine tables in the whole place you really need to book in advance. Afterwards we always go to the Bongo Club. Super scruffy but loads of fun, there's a really laid back vibe and a mixed crowd. They have a different style on every night and you're guaranteed a good time no matter what's on."

See The Locals' Directory on page 136 for Fiona's top tips.

Despite changeable weather conditions and freezing cold winters, outdoor drinking is more popular than ever. Here are the beer gardens worth visiting...

The sheer size of **The Peartree** beer garden makes it a magnet for boozy sun worshippers. Its proximity to the University ensures a decent student crowd and the long benches makes it all the easier to mingle with other drinkers (38 West Nicolson St, Old Town, Map A5).

The Cumberland Bar's beer garden is just below street level, shaded by trees set amongst the tables. Join the post-work crowds and get your drinks in before it gets too busy. The chilled and friendly atmosphere makes this bar one of the best outdoor spots in the city (1-3 Cumberland St, New Town, Map B3).

Finish off a stroll around the Royal Botanic Gardens with a well earned drink at the back of the **Botanic House Hotel**. Don't let the quiet bar put you off – everyone's outside basking in the sunshine. Slightly off the beaten track, this is the place to go to when all other beer gardens are overflowing (27 Inverleith Row, Inverleith, Map C1).

Sandwiched between two student areas, Marchmont and Bruntsfield, **The Links Hotel and Bar** has an opportunistic beer garden to attract those fresh off the Meadows and Bruntsfield links. Summer barbeques and large screens for sport keep the crowds happy, even if the sun goes in (4 Alvanley Terrace, Whitehouse Loan, Marchmont, Map C7). –

Everybody needs good neighbours. Where better to find them than down the local? We've picked a handful of pubs that have been recommended by those living nearby.

Affluent Stockbridge has found a home in **Hector's**. This funky style bar has a constant buzz as a local crowd is joined by well heeled thirty-somethings and older patrons. Unbeatable breakfasts and a modern but low key design makes this welcoming bar worth a visit (47-49 Deanhaugh St, Stockbridge, Map D3).

Like Marmite, you'll either love or hate the **Canny Man's**. Supporters cite the staggering amount of artefacts hanging from the walls and the homely feel of a

♩Thistle Street Bar ♭The Waverley ♫Brass Monkey ♮The Cumberland Bar

♩Hector's ♭Canny Man's ♯The Shore Bar ♪Port O'Leith

pub run with some very unconventional rules (a booklet of the local law is available at the bar). Those against will refer to those draconian measures and standoffish staff. Whatever side of the fence you sit on, the Canny Man's is a truly unique Edinburgh experience and an absolute must (237 Morningside Rd, Morningside, Map D8).

Henricks caters for the pre-dinner and neighbourhood crowds. Its tasteful interior sports Persian rugs and chandeliers without feeling too much like a boudoir (1 Barclay Pl, Bruntsfield, Map C6).

A wee maritime gem with huge mirrors set behind crescent seating spaces, **The Shore Bar** has live music on Tuesdays, Wednesdays and Saturdays. The restaurant is a regular entrant in the Good Food Guide and on sunny days the outdoor tables take the pub to the neighbourhood (3 Shore, Leith, beyond Map A1).

From the port to the pond, these choices are Edinburgh's unmissables...

Leith's best known sailors' pub is an assault on the senses. Stepping inside the **Port O' Leith**, the ceiling is adorned with flags, the walls covered with maritime paraphernalia and the sound provided by Leith FM Radio and the occasional jukebox tune. The atmosphere here can range from an episode of Twin Peaks to a Leith-style version of the party film Coyote Ugly (58 Constitution St, Leith, beyond Map A1).

Home to Ian Rankin and his fictional detective Rebus, **The Oxford Bar** is now a place of pilgrimage. Don't let that put you off though. The bar stools are home to regulars, with many visitors exploring the backroom but missing out on the craic in the process. Find a stool and settle in for the night (8 Young St, New Town, Map C4).

The Sheep Heid Inn has been around since 1360, making it Scotland's oldest surviving public house. A cosy traditional pub with a beer garden and a unique skittle alley attached, this place offers the best cold pints for walkers stepping outside the city (43-45 The Causeway, Duddingston. Take bus 4 or 44 from Princes St plus a 10 min walk, or bus 42 from Hanover St which will drop you at the end of the street. Alternatively walk from the foot of Arthur's Seat, 30 mins approx).

Step inside **Oloroso**. Yes it's a restaurant. Yes it has a bar and, yes, the staff here make the finest Bloody Marys in the city. With stunning views of the Castle, this home of luxury dining mightn't seem the like the best place to arrive with your scruffy hangover but for those who do, the greatest cure awaits (33 Castle St, New Town, Map C4).

For impromptu folk sessions, fine ales and a warm welcome from the regulars you can't beat **Sandy Bell's**. An Edinburgh institution, this narrow pub makes the most of its space, cramming in punters for a cracking atmosphere (25 Forrest Rd, Old Town, Map B5).

Save the best for last. On the outskirts of the city and a stone's throw away from Leith's red light district lies the jewel in Edinburgh's pub crown. **The Pond** is an eclectic venue, with possibly the finest bar snack selection anywhere in the city. The chilli pickled eggs are for the strongest stomachs only, but to wash them down there's a great selection of wheat beers (including a rotating guest beer every couple of weeks). Tropical fish are amongst the regulars here and other treats include the old style arcade version of Space Invaders in the back room. The Pond has been described as the perfect day-after-the-night before pub. Just make sure you spent the night before there as well (2-4 Bath Rd, off Salamander St, Leith, beyond Map A1).

Sandy Bell's The Pond Oloroso

John takes a break from his work on a listed greenhouse

Learn more about Jock Tamson's Bairns on their website www.jtbairns.com
Their latest CD, Rare, is released on Greentrax Recordings label

INTERVIEW:
John Croall
(joiner & folk musician)

" I got into joinery as soon as I left school. The wonderful thing about the job is to have the skills to bring old things back to life. We live in a society where nothing gets repaired and everything is disposable – but joinery gives me the opportunity to say 'yes, I can fix that!'. One of the projects I'm most proud of is the conservation of a 19th century listed greenhouse near the Botanic Gardens. My men and I have worked on it a few times over the years, four or five days of craftsmanship are enough to keep it in shape for another good decade.

Edinburgh has fine examples of timber and architecture going together. The Queen's Gallery in the Palace of Holyroodhouse features a stunning ceiling and beautiful double staircase. You can tell the joinery has followed traditional methods; the bends are cut and shaped out of massive pieces of timber, which is a wonderful thing to see.

My other great passion is music. I have been playing Scottish folk music with Jock Tamson's Bairns band since the 1970s. We get asked to play abroad every now and then, which is wonderful, and sometimes we perform at The Edinburgh Folk Club, a regular Wednesday event at the Pleasance. During the rest of the week the place to catch some folk is Sandy Bell's – some nights you'll catch the fiddle, other nights it'll be the pipes, nowadays you get some singing as well.

My local pub is the Links Tavern which can only be described as a bit of a spit-and-sawdust place and newcomers might find it a little peculiar. Nowadays the tavern allows women in, but when I first went there 30 years ago they were not, as the landlord said, 'encouraged'. Any woman who goes there now still needs to ask for a key to the toilets.

The other place I go to regularly is Domenico's, a wonderful and small family-run Italian restaurant near the Shore in Leith. There are so many nice restaurants along the waterfront, I would recommend anyone new to the city to come down here for dinner. "

See The Locals' Directory on page 136 for John's top tips.
John Croall joinery services can be reached on t: 0131 553 4315.

The night is young. The night is always young. Edinburgh might not be known as the city that never sleeps but before you do head to bed here's where to party across town. Club nights and regular gig slots mainly fall in four week cycles so don't always expect the same tunes every week. To give you a flavour of Edinburgh nightlife we've picked out some of the city's most popular venues and what goes on in them.

Breakin' beats, drum'n'bass, reggae, indie, funk, hip-hop and house are just some of the styles and sounds emanating from Edinburgh's original multi arts venue, **The Bongo Club**. Based in Edinburgh University's Moray House the venue attracts a friendly mixed crowd. There's no stress about jeans and trainers here as the rough and ready space deserves a good dressing down. Nights everybody's talking about include the long running Headspin – a feast of visuals frame floor filling sets of funk, hip-hop electro and house (Moray House, Holyrood Rd, Old Town, Map A4).

Slippery when wet, the **Liquid Rooms** is a low down dirty venue. Deep in an underground cavern some of the greatest acts have performed here including the Smashing Pumpkins, Moby, Ice T and the Kaiser Chiefs. Club nights have continually pushed the boundaries of the alternative music scene and created a cult reputation for the venue. Long running weekly night Evol sandwiches indie, alternative and pop-rock, and the legendary Luvely is a home for house lovers every month (9c Victoria St, Old Town, Map B5).

New kid on the block **Cabaret Voltaire** is the baby of the bunch. Open in its current guise since 2002, it quickly established a reputation for being one of the city's most electric venues. These underground vaults have the feel of an illicit bolthole and when full to bursting you wouldn't want to be anywhere else. Long running club nights now hosted here include: gay friendly vocal garage and deep house Taste (weekly), house spectacular Ultragroove (twice monthly) and the monthly freestyle funkfest that is Trouble (36 Blair St, Old Town, Map A4).

A dancehall from 1918, **Club Ego** retains some of this old world charm even if it's a little shabby around the edges (so would you if you'd been about that long!). Without doubt the most eclectic club in terms of musical styles, Ego hosts the award winning Vegas of swing, lounge jazz and ratpack tunes (monthly). Also monthly, live music meets clubbing carnival with the 8 piece excesses of Tokyoblu's garage, house, disco, funk, gospel and electro beats (14 Picardy Pl, near Broughton St, Map A3).

The city's **live music** scene caters for all tastes. Get high on folk at Sandy Bell's for impromptu sessions (most evenings) and catch regular gigs at The Royal Oak on Infirmary Street or The Edinburgh Folk Club at the Pleasance Cabaret Bar (Wednesdays). Swing by the Coda Music shop on North Bank Street to find out what's on where with traditional music events. Lounge lizards and jazz hands can choose between Henry's Cellar Bar on Morrison Street and the ever-changing line ups at The Jazz Bar on Chambers Street. For the best new music across the city keep an eye out for Baby Tiger events (www.babytigermusic.com) and check out the line ups at Studio 24, Cabaret Voltaire and Whistlebinkies. Established acts can perform anywhere from the compact Liquid Rooms, the 3000 capacity Corn Exchange, the Playhouse Theatre or the The Queen's Hall.

Be a local! Buy **The List Magazine** to find out what's on where, or just wander into Ripping Records on South Bridge to pick up tickets for any gig in the city.

INTERVIEW:
Trendy Wendy
(dj & girl about town)

Trendy Wendy, co-owner of The Street bar and host of numerous club nights including the long running Tackno and the Playgirl Mansion nights, has become infamous as "Edinburgh's party girl."

When I started DJing in the mid-nineties there were very few clubs. There are lots of places now but it's still changing – there are places constantly closing down and new places opening up. It's a small scene but diverse enough, there's quite a bit going on even with the smoking ban hitting the clubs' business.

For music I go to the HMV store on Princes Street, they've got a great vinyl record selection. And Cockburn Street is another good spot: Underground Solu'shun is a really popular shop with DJs, and Fopp on Rose Street is great for cheap CDs. For buying art I really recommend The Red Door Gallery: they sell an interesting mix of pieces, all quite fresh and affordable.

Cabaret Voltaire is one of my favourite clubs. No matter what night you pick you get good music; on Fridays and Saturdays you'll catch guest DJs from all over the world. It's a great venue: just the right size, intimate enough, and earlier in the night they have excellent live music on. I do go to Ego quite a lot; it's just around the corner from my own bar. And right now Lulu is the best purpose-built club in Edinburgh and I love DJing there, their glass-lit dance floor is such a fun feature.

I do late nights so I love my brunch and Hector's Bar is one of my favourites – it's a beautiful setting, delicious food and perfect Bloody Marys. Sometimes I go to Villager for a light lunch – the menu is creative and the environment chilled out.

But if you're after some luxury then head to The Witchery. It's something unique to Edinburgh, a hotel set in a 16th century merchant house. Have a meal in the Secret Garden restaurant and stay in one of their rooms for the complete experience. You will feel like royalty, it's really decadent and dramatic."

See The Locals' Directory on page 136 for Wendy's top tips.
Check www.playgirlmansions.co.uk for news on Wendy's gigs,
find her at The Street, 2 Picardy Pl, New Townish, Map A3.

Wendy plays another floor filler at Lulu

fest
ival
fever

Edinburgh in August. All five festivals clamour to get your attention. The population doubles as tens of thousands flock to 'Athens of the North' for a slice of culture. Accommodation prices skyrocket, it's a challenge to get a table in even the shabbiest restaurant and the city is mobbed. Yet you can't help but be drawn into Edinburgh's festival fever.

Here's our top tips to get the most out of the season:

Seek out the unusual venues

Shows have taken place in public toilets, a lift, hotel rooms, underground caverns, church halls and even an upside down cow. Every year new spaces are discovered and while the quality of shows on offer is never guaranteed, the venue can often pull off the best performance.

Take a chance with a random choice

The star review system can be a minefield, with dozens of publications pointing you in different directions. Sometimes the best way to make up your mind is to walk randomly into the first show you come across. Many festival goers plan their trips like military operations, with every minute of every day accounted for. But to fully embrace the festival atmosphere a spontaneous approach is best.

Talk to the taxi drivers

Just like a day at the races, some people have the inside track. What Wikipedia won't know and Google can't find will be behind the wheel of a black cab. Hot-wired to all the latest festival gossip and recommendations, it's worth quizzing your driver if they're up for a chat. And all good tips deserve the same in return…

Drink up, it's closing time

As well as an influx of short term venues, the city finds space for numerous temporary bars. The latest you can get a pint is 5am, before an early morning pub opens again at 6am. Use your time to explore underground caves (Baby Belly Bar, Niddry St South, Map A5), a University Library (Gilded Balloon Library Bar, Teviot Row House, Bristo Sq, Map B5), the leafy surrounds of a garden (Speigel Bar, George Sq Gardens, Map B5), old bank vaults (Jelly Belly and Beer Belly Bars, Cowgate, Map B5) or even share a heavenly pint with the man upstairs in the organic church bar (Assembly @ St George's West, Shandwick Pl, Map D4).

Celeb spotting

Who needs Hollywood when you've got Holyrood? Navigate your way past the eager students thrusting flyers into your face and you might catch a glimpse of fame on foot. Edinburgh in August has it all. A mix of British soap star has-beens, Hollywood legends (Sir Sean Connery sees fit to return most years) and international celebs (most of whom are blissfully invisible here). You can try to blag your way into the members-only bars to rub shoulders with the anointed, but you're much better off taking to the streets to track down the talent. The greatest kudos goes to the future celeb spotter, those that might have seen Hugh Grant in a church hall in 1985, Robin Williams in The Taming of the Shrew in 1978, or a ballsy Emma Thompson as part of the Cambridge Footlights in 1980. So who knows where that talented student actor will end up, it might be worth getting that autograph now…

get away from it all

The intensity of the festival is best enjoyed in between some well-earned breaks

Go Green

The Edinburgh International Book Festival **(Map D4)** provides a welcome antidote to the madness on the streets: its tented complex on Charlotte Square Gardens is a picture of tranquility. No musicians banging drums, no harassment from performers, just stimulating talks and great ice-cream. For another green escape head to the Royal Botanic Gardens **(Map D2)**, grab a takeaway coffee and view the city centre from a park bench (if you exit the gardens via Inverleith Row check out the beer garden at The Botanic House Hotel, Map C1).

On Your Bike

Or rent a bike and head to Cramond village, 4 miles west of the city (rent from Cycle Scotland, 29 Blackfriars St, t: 0131 556 5560). You can pick up the Roseburn Cycle Path at Wester Coates Terrace (which is off West Coates, the road that heads out to the airport from Haymarket Terrace). Once on the path, head north. Soon after passing under Queensferry Road, turn half left at the Sustrans marker to join the Blackhall Path. The path ends a mile later near Silverknowes Road and you can cycle down that road till you reach the water. Turn left at the water and follow the esplanade all the way to the River Almond Walkaway. You've arrived!

Other Escapes

A quick jaunt up Arthur's Seat, some quiet time in the Mushroom Garden off the Royal Mile at Dunbar's Close or a seaside stroll along Portobello Beach, **(take bus 12 or 15 from Princes St)** will all recharge your festival batteries enough to party hard all over again on your return.

Scotland

It was a day peculiar to this piece of the planet,
when larks rose on long thin strings of singing
and the air shifted with the shimmer of actual angels.
Greenness entered the body. The grasses
shivered with presences, and sunlight
stayed like a halo on hair and heather and hills.
Walking into town, I saw, in a radiant raincoat,
the woman from the fish-shop. 'What a day it is!'
cried I, like a sunstruck madman.
And what did she have to say for it?
Her brow grew bleak, her ancestors raged in their graves
and she spoke with their ancient misery:

'We'll pay for it,
we'll pay for it,
we'll pay for it!'

Alastair Reid

Off the beaten attractions

Skip the queues and discover some of the lesser known treasures in Scotland's capital.

St Mary's Cathedral

Avoid the tourist crowds at St Giles' on the Royal Mile and pay a visit to the awesome St Mary's Cathedral. Completed in 1879, this imposing neo-gothic building has three unique spires instantly recognisable as part of Edinburgh's skyline. Approach from Melville Street to fully appreciate the sheer magnitude of Scotland's largest cathedral erected since the Reformation. Inside, the breathtaking flying buttresses supporting the main 270ft spire are an architechtural wonder and art enthusiasts can enjoy the celebrated collection of paintings. On a sunny day catch the colourful reflections of Eduardo Paolozzi's impressive stained glass window in the Resurrection chapel. Guided tours can be organised in advance (Palmerston Pl, West End, t: 0131 225 6293, Map D4).

The Edinburgh Labyrinth

Take time out and tread the path of Scotland's only permanent labyrinth. Situated in the northwest corner of George Square Gardens, The Edinburgh Labyrinth is a chance to slow down and still the mind. Not to be confused with a maze riddled with dizzying dead ends, labyrinths have only one clear path to follow, for when you need to shut out all distractions and take a moment to reflect. This 13th century design, based on the original at Chartres Cathedral in France, is the perfect way to unwind – going round and round in circles is finally a good thing! (George Sq, Old Town, Map B5)

Ferry to Inchcolm Island

Known as 'The Iona of the East' Inchcolm island makes an excellent day trip. Catch the Maid of Forth Ferry from South Queensferry or Newhaven and look out for grey seals, puffins and, on a good day, dolphins and porpoises. Enjoy a spectacular view of Edinburgh across the Forth whilst picknicking on the beach. Pass the champagne dahling! (Running from Jun to Oct, log on to www.maidofforth.co.uk or t: 0131 331 5000 for details).

Edinburgh Printmakers

Once the beacon of the printing and publishing industry, Edinburgh's history is alive and well at Edinburgh Printmakers, Britain's first open access art studio. Visitors have the chance to see the workings of this co-operative, take classes in printmaking and purchase the work of local artists. Unlike commercial galleries, proceeds from every sale go directly to the artist and/or the organisation (Union St, just off the top of Leith Walk, tue to sat, Map A3).

Surgeons' Hall Museum

Not for the faint of heart or queasy of stomach, the bizzare and brilliant exhibits at Surgeons' Hall Museum are a must see. Edinburgh's place in medical history is preserved here along with body parts in formaldehyde, historic medical charts and a grisly selection of surgical implements. This atmosphere is straight out of a Sherlock Holmes novel - not surprising as the fictional detective was modelled on the brilliant mind of the one time College of Surgeons President, Joseph Bell. The reasons to go are elementary (Nicolson St, Southside, www.rcsed.ac.uk, closed weekends, t: 0131 527 1600, Map A5).

INTERVIEW:
Ruth Kirkpatrick

(storyteller)

'Once upon a time I went for lunch at Sadivino'

Ruth's decision to return to Scotland helped develop her natural flair for storytelling. Being in Edinburgh really opened her appetite for Scottish stories, particularly the gusty tales from the traveller tradition.

❝ Scotland has a great tradition of oral storytelling. To enjoy some you should go to Guid Crack, a club that meets on the last Friday of every month at The Waverley Bar. It is really informal and friendly, just a lovely bunch of people who get together to tell stories live – anyone is welcome to go and listen to them.

And, of course, céilidhs (traditional Scottish dances) are such good fun! The people from the Adult Learning Project do a very good céilidh once a month, in the St Bride's Centre on Gorgie Road. I love taking my friends there. Don't worry if it is your first time, they are very good at explaining the steps.

If there's one thing I make sure I never miss every year it's the Steiner School Christmas Fair. My friends have flown in from London especially, it is that good! Steiner's is such an artistic school, their crafts are beautifully designed and of incredible quality. The building is transformed with lights and fairy-tale rooms which really capture the breathtaking scenery of a white winter.

Whatever time of the year it is you'll always find me at Sadivino, my favourite café in Edinburgh. Carmen and Alessandro, who run it, worked in Edinburgh restaurants for years and now bring their Italian and Spanish roots to the food. On a sunny day you can take one of the tables outside and gaze up at Salisbury Crags. It is such a stunning view.

There are so many great things to do near Edinburgh if you feel like venturing out a bit. The Traquair Fayre in Traquair House (near Peebles) is a lovely summer festival. It is set in the landscaped gardens of a grand 12th century home where Bonnie Prince Charles spent the night. The house brews its own beer and a lot of the street acts of the Edinburgh Festival Fringe perform there first. There is food and a camp site – it attracts a bit of an alternative crowd and is an excellent thing to do if you have children."

See The Locals' Directory on page 136 for Ruth's top tips.
For a storytelling session email Ruth at ruth@storiesallways.co.uk

arnardo's 110

JottyKin

1930's

BIG IDEAS

SWEETS

elte

25

lker
Slater

VALVONA & C

what's in stores?

Edinburgh is a city for explorers. In typical understated fashion the treasures of the city, much like the wealth of its residents, are not for public display. Scratch beneath the surface though and discover shopping riches. You won't find the blindingly obvious any-town stores on these pages. Instead, we've shunned the high street to highlight retail paradise spots unique to Edinburgh. High end boutiques, local designers, chaotic bookshops, independent music stores, valuable vintage finds and the charity shop trail give Edinburgh a retail geography unlike any other city. Turn the pages for our treasure map. X marks the spots...

When it comes to stepping out in style here are the lines, whichs and wardrobes we recommend getting lost in...

Going solo has never been such a good idea. **Solo Menswear** on the Royal Mile is a stylish independent store for men keen to make a well-dressed impression. With labels from London and abroad, there's a mix of smart casual with the odd killer number thrown in (276 Canongate, Old Town, Map A4).

Telling it like is, **Totty Rocks** is the retro chic creation of Holly Campbell and Lynsey Miller who are interviewed on page 114. Their designs focus on reinventing classic looks with funky twists. There's a wee selection of men's clothes also and some damn fine accessories to rock your totty (40 Victoria St, Old Town, Map B5).

Edinburgh mightn't be Milan but to dress straight from the Italian fashion capital's streets make sure you seek out **Sprio**. Tucked in a basement space underneath a café of the same name, its owners moved from Italy and took what they loved best with them. Check out the great selection of ladies shoes and fine italian fabrics, all at affordable prices (37 St Stephen St, Stockbridge, Map C3).

Suits you sir. **Peter Johnston** should know. This former head of design at Dunhill has brought a slice of Savile Row to the capital. Top quality made-to -measure suits and shirts are his speciality, and ladies are treated to similarly elegant designs. Peter's store in the Grassmarket is as understated and elegant as his tailoring (81 Grassmarket, Old Town, Map B5).

If your wallet is just burning a hole in your pocket you can well and truly douse those flames in **Corniche**. A boutique for the label hunters; Vivienne Westwood, Yohji Yamamoto et al rub shoulders with the finest up and coming Scottish designers. You'll leave out of pocket, but what a pocket! (2 Jeffrey St, Old Town, Map A4)

Sam Thomas on the corner of Stafford Street has been key to the revival of West End Boutique shopping. Labels include Avoca, Inwear, Viln and Uttam with a variety of prices to suit every shopper. These are supplemented by an eye-catching array of jewellery, handbags and shoes in her adjoining accessories store (18 Stafford St, West End, Map D4).

■Totty Rocks ■Sam Thomas ■Corniche

INTERVIEW:
Holly & Lynsey
(fashion designers & retro chicks)

Lynsey and Holly get ready to Rock N' Bowl

Holly Campbell and Lynsey Miller founded fashion and accessory label Totty Rocks in 2004. Two years later they opened their own boutique offering both womenswear and menswear ranges. All garments are designed on the premises and made in Scotland.

Edinburgh has changed so much since 2002 - we have a lot more shops now but there's still room for smaller retailers. We would love more people to do what we have done and open their own independent boutiques as it would add to the diversity of the city.

Both of us are passionate about the city and the fashion scene evolving within it. We love vintage finds and individual shops. The Grassmarket area offers fantastic choice from clothing to cheese and wine, fancy dress, crafts, books and much more. There are lots of inspirational places to be found if you're in the mood for vintage rummaging; go to Ingliston Antique Fair or Sam Burn's in Cockenzie, right next to Prestonpans. Holly just bought an ironing board there; it's pre-war and completely indestructible! There's also a brilliant shop in Causewayside called Allan Jackson Antique and Curios which is a haven of hidden treasures.

Because we spend so much time working on the business, we love to eat out as a well-earned treat. There's a fantastic Turkish restaurant on St Mary's Street called Empire; their tiny upstairs room is so warm and friendly. Lynsey's favourite Thai restaurant is Dusit, it's one of the best curries in town!

If you're in the mood for lounging, eating good food with a huge range of exciting cocktails, then you could kick back and relax in Villager on George IV Bridge all day. For a real organic breakfast there's no better place than Urban Angel in Hanover Street, their Stornoway Black pudding is the best on the planet!

We love getting dressed up and going out dancing. The Bongo Club does a fantastic country music club night called Ride This Train and The Citrus Club does a brilliant 80's night on a Friday. If we're feeling particularly energetic nothing beats bowling in the winter. We sometimes go to Megabowl in Fountainbridge but for a real nostalgic experience try The Sheep Heid Inn in Duddingston. It has its own skittle alley that you can make a group booking for."

See The Locals' Directory on page 137 for Holly and Lynsey's top tips.
Totty Rocks, 40 Victoria St, Old Town, Map A4.

THE CHRISTMAS SHOP

Victoria Street

■Concrete Wardrobe ▯Joey D's ▯Chic & Unique

A cut above the commoner casual options, these shopping spots combine funky flair with some elegant slumming...

Rip it up and start again by stepping into **Joey Ds**. This Edinburgh institution has transformed scraps of old jeans, jackets, slacks, suits – anything and everything, into some of the funkiest clothing for guys and girls. For those in search of the perfect gift this designer's handbags are iconic sure fire hits (54 Broughton St, New Townish, Map B3).

Nestled on West Port below the art college, **Godiva** hosts a mix of vintage finds, new work from fashion graduates and reworked classics. If it's all too much to take in then feel free to chill on their wee Chesterfield couch while you survey the purchasing possibilities. Split into two rooms, there are enough guys and girls champion choices to keep you busy for a while (9 West Port, Old Town, Map C5).

Full of fresh fashion and hip home solutions, **Concrete Wardrobe** is a well-stocked larder of the best in Scottish design talent. Whether dressing to impress or making designs on a new home, it's worth spending the extra pennies here (50a Broughton St, New Town, Map B3).

It's Scottish but not as you know it. The traditional kilt gets a makeover by designer Howie Nicholsby at **21st Century Kilts**. Adorned by celebrites such as Vin Diesel, Alan Cumming and KT Tunstall, Howie's designs have been shot by Mario Testino, graced the Playboy Mansion and lauded by fashionistas in New York. Whether it's in leather, pinstripe or any of the other funky designs make sure you're dressed to kilt (57 High St, Royal Mile, Old Town, Map A4).

There's no better present than the past and Edinburgh's vintage stores are full of memories from days gone by with clothes and accessories that certainly haven't. Find the finest in these top time travelling tips.

Elaine's Vintage Clothing ranges from 1900 to the 1970s and this intimate wee shop is the place to go for second-hand ball gowns, capes, coats, feather boas, silk blouses and waistcoats. Try not to be distracted by the fab vintage posters, back issues of Vogue and old LPs while you peruse the selection on show (55 St Stephen St, Stockbridge, Map C3).

A haven for retro romantics, **Herman Brown's** window seems like an oasis amongst strip bars and greasy chippys. Stocking retro to modern clothing, a kooky and quirky array of vintage jewellery and some breathtaking 1920s dresses, this store is worth seeking out (151 West Port, Old Town, Map C5).

If you've found the perfect outfit but still feel it's lacking something, then Moira Teal might be able to help. The owner of **Chic & Unique** has a staggering range of hand picked costume and vintage jewellery mainly from the 1950s and before. Gents make sure you check out the ace cufflink selection (8 Deanhaugh St, Stockbridge, Map D3).

Charity begins at home but is much more stylish at **Barnardos Vintage** in the Grassmarket. The first foray of a charity shop into the vintage scene, its stock is sourced from all eighteen Barnardos stores in the city. As well as a selection of items for men and women, a dress and evening wear hire service is also available (116 West Bow, Old Town, Map B5).

The grand daddys of the vintage scene are **W.M. Armstrong's** (81-83 Grassmarket, Old Town, Map B5). The flagship store in the Grassmarket hosts a cornucopia of delights through the decades and is a tourist attraction in its own right. If the superb selection of stuff gets you pining for more make sure you get to their sister stores, the **Rusty Zip** (14 Teviot Pl, Old Town, Map B5) near Edinburgh University and the other **Armstrong's** store (64-66 Clerk St, Southside, Map A6).

Pick up a good deal at one of the city's 90+ charity shops. To whet your appetite here are the most - see shops from our bargain hunting experts.

It mightn't look like much from the outside but the inside of **Hospice for Hope Romania** in Tollcross is full of retail finds and the source of many a funky dress. Bright and more spacious than most charity shops, the friendly staff are always keen to aid your search (62 Home St, Tollcross, Map C6).

■ Armstrong's ◧ Herman Brown's ◧ Barnardos Vintage

🎵Unicorn Antiques 🎵Hospice for Hope 🎵Meadows Lamp Gallery 🎵Georgian Antiques

For a complete mixed bag seek out **Shelter on Forrest Road**. Brooches, old cameras, retro trainers, handbags and CDs clamour for your attention. Its close proximity to Edinburgh University ensures a great selection of young and funky clothes and accessories (39 Forrest Rd, Old Town, Map B5).

As one of the original charity shops, Oxfam was first to open speciality branches. Amongst the slew of stores in Stockbridge, **Oxfam Bookshop** and **Oxfam Music** are run by enthusiasts whose passion shines through in eye catching window displays. There's a great selection of titles in both and for those who want to hold on to their redundant records there's an LP framing option in Oxfam Music! (25 and 64 Raeburn Pl, Stockbridge, Map D3)

Similar to its sister shop on Forrest Road, **Shelter in Stockbridge** is stuffed to the gills with all kinds of everything. Where its Old Town branch has a focus on young and funky stock, the affluent neighbourhood is reflected here with some great quality knits, many of the 50s cashmere variety! (106a Raeburn Pl, Stockbridge, Map D3)

For a treasure map of all charity shops call Changeworks on 0131 538 7943 or find it on their website at www.changeworks.org.uk (search for 'Charity Shop').

Thinking of taking some history home with you? Start shopping here... **XXX**

Some of the most elegant residences in Marchmont, Morningside and Bruntsfield are well-lit wonders thanks to the **Meadows Lamp Gallery**. The breathtaking selection of art nouveau lighting pieces are mainly sourced from local homes and sold on to local customers. Stop by on a Tuesday, Thursday or Saturday and catch a glimpse of old Edinburgh grandeur (48 Warrender Park Rd, Marchmont, Map B6).

Not for the clumsy, **Unicorn Antiques** is a compact upstairs/downstairs treasure trove in the New Town. The higgledy piggledy arrangement of curios and antiques gives a casual browsing atmosphere with prices to suit all budgets. An explorer's paradise (65 Dundas St, New Town, Map C3).

The Red Door Gallery Present Armchair Books

Visting **Georgian Antiques** in Leith is like stepping into a museum. Set in a converted whisky bond, 50,000sq ft of space is dedicated to Scotland's largest collection of quality antiques. Give yourself an afternoon off and be guided through the incredible selection by the friendly staff on hand (10 Pattison St, off Leith Links, Leith, beyond Map A2).

Shops that stock outside the bo**X** derserve a mention here...

Steer clear of the Royal Mile's tartan tat at **Present**: it's full of quirky and fun designer ideas for life, from retro phones to funky wall decorations. You'll arrive present shopping for a friend but won't be able to resist looking after yourself and leaving with two of everything! (26 St Mary's St, Old Town, Map A4)

Off the beaten path on West Port is **Armchair Books**, an old school second hand bookstore which looks like it was built entirely of books. Enjoy the musty smell all bookshops should have and get lost in the nooks and crannies of this reader's retreat, famous for their selection of Victorian titles (72-74 West Port, Old Town, Map C5).

What to buy, books or CDs? Can't decide? Then get down to **Elvis Shakespeare** on Leith Walk. A specialist dealer in rare vinyl and quality literature, this classic combo shop even has coffee available to browsers who want to spend a bit of time looking through the selections available. The Bard and the King would have approved (347 Leith Walk, Leith, beyond Map A2).

Avalanche on Cockburn Street sells a wide selection of CDs, DVDs and vinyl; you might even catch the odd gig crammed in between the 7" racks. Local artists are also stocked here if you're keen to get a taste of the city's latest talent (63 Cockburn St, Old Town, Map B4).

Affordable art abounds in **The Red Door Gallery**, a showcase store for the city's established and emerging artists. Contemporary work includes prints, photographs, accessories and mixed media (42 Victoria St, Old Town, Map B5).

INTERVIEW:
Lisa
(reader, sportswoman, schoolgirl)

Lisa's loves books; reading is her number one hobby. A keen sportswoman she also plays for her school's football team.

My time is mostly spent doing sport and arty stuff. I play hockey, football, netball and tennis. I really enjoy going to the rugby and have been to Murrayfield to watch Scotland play. We go down there to see the matches but also to go iceskating on the rink.

Paperchase is a great shop to buy scrapbooks, art pencils and other things to draw with. I like having lots of different notebooks to draw things from the books I read. I have read nearly 100 books over the year - sometimes I read several at a time.

Waterstone's in George Street is one of my favourite places in Edinburgh. You can read in the shop and it even has a café with really good almond croissants. When we moved to Edinburgh we went there every Sunday. My mum says I thought it was a library, not a bookshop, because I just walked around and picked whatever book I wanted.

The Museum of Scotland is good. They have a section on animals, the ones that are extinct but also the ones that still exist today, and a section on science where you can drive a racing car. And the Museum of Childhood is very nice too. It has all these toys – the first toys that were made and you can see how they changed and came to be the toys we have today."

et: Toys from Museum of Childhood & National Museum of Scotland

Lisa gets lost in Waterstone's

O my Luve's like a red, red rose,
That's newly sprung in June;
O my Luve's like the melodie
That's sweetly play'd in tune.

As fair art thou, my bonie lass,
So deep in luve am I;
And I will luve thee still, my Dear,
Till a' the seas gang dry.

(From My Luve is Like a Red, Red Rose by Robert Burns)

Romantic
Edinburgh

It's no wonder Robert Burns, a poet known for his many conquests, felt at home in Edinburgh. At every turn the city reveals breathtaking views or hidden spots to woo even the most hardened of hearts. These are our top five amorous locations.

Scotsman Hotel Screenings

This isn't just any old date to the cinema. The seasonal Sunday night schedule favours the colder months and is a must for lovers of classic movies. Log onto their website (www.scotsmanscreenings.com) or buy your tickets at the hotel - choose from the options of gourmet dinner and a movie or just the straight screening (20 North Bridge, Old Town, t: 0131 556 5565, Map B4).

Canal Boat Canoodling

Take to the canal and hire a row boat from the Edinburgh Canal Society. It's just off Ashley Terrace (Morningside). The best way to get there is to head to Edinburgh Quay (Map D6) in Fountainbridge and follow the water. Open between 11am and 5pm on Sundays, on a good day it's an absolute must. At just a few pounds for every romantic hour you have the chance to impress with your rowing skills or drift downstream while you try and figure out how to get back.

Ramsay Gardens Bench

Just below the Castle is a lone bench looking out to the New Town, a perfect spot for enjoying the beauty of the city without being surrounded by others. It stands beneath Ramsay Gardens (which is not a garden, but the name of the 18th century residential white buildings to the left of the Castle). The best way to get there is by going through Princes Street Gardens: follow the paths behind the Ross Bandstand and cross the railway track over the bridge. Then walk the zigzag paths up to the other side and you'll be at the north side of the Castle. You have arrived at your bench. Don't get too caught up in the privacy though - you're still in full view of everybody on the other side of town (Map C4).

The Royal Observatory

Take a break from gazing into each others eyes and stare at the skies at night instead. Scotland has some of the darkest skies in Europe, offering spectacular views of the stars and the planets. On Fridays you can join the Observing Evenings at the Royal Observatory on Blackford Hill (7pm start time). Make sure to book in advance though by calling **0131 668 8404**. Check out the latest details on www.roe.ac.uk/vc

A Roof with a View

Rooftop romance abounds at The Tower. Let your hair down Rapunzel style as you quaff champagne on the restaurant's outdoor terrace. The icing on the cake of the Museum of Scotland, The Tower Restaurant (Chambers St, Old Town, Map B5, t: 0131 225 3003) offers stunning views of the Castle and the city's skyline providing the perfect backdrop to an amorous evening. Whether to dine or to drink, time spent there will be one piece of history you'll never forget.

And if you can't get enough of that loving feeling: try fine dining at The Witchery (page 21), a romantic stroll from Stockbridge to the National Gallery of Modern Art along the Water of Leith (page 66) or the breathtaking views on Calton Hill (just 5 minutes from the East End of Princes St, Map A4).

A dreich winter evening on the Royal Mile

No Money

Only got a few sweets and some fluff in those pockets? Nae worries. Here's some cheap thrills in the land of the free...

Pitch up on the edge of The Meadows for 36 holes of gratis greens and free fairways at the Pitch 'n' Putt course on Bruntsfield Links. The Oldest Short Hole Golf Course in the world (since 1895) is the perfect way to spend a summer's afternoon. Playing badly is as much fun as playing well – watch out for people on the footpaths! If you don't have the kit it will cost a few quid at The Golf Tavern to rent (or free with your lunch) (30-31 Wright's Houses, Bruntsfield, Map C6).

Opened amid controversy over escalating costs in 2004, the award-winning Scottish Parliament Building at Holyrood is fast becoming one of the city's busiest attractions. Designed by Enric Miralles, the impressive structure reflects the majesty of Salisbury Crags and Arthur's Seat. Visitors can tour the building and watch Scottish politics in action from the debating chamber, when parliament is in session (Holyrood, Old Town, t: 0131 348 5200, beyond Map A4).

Inspired by gigs organised by KT Tunstall in 2001, Acoustic Edinburgh was founded by Paul Gilbody and Simon Kirby as a regular monthly event to showcase the best original music coming out of Scotland. Happening on the first Tuesday of every month, musical styles range from laid back lazy cool, funky latin grooves, african beats, satirical folk, stunning guitar wizardry and much more. Check out www.acousticedinburgh.com for the latest listings (Medina Nightclub, 45-47, Lothian St, near Teviot Pl, Old Town, Map B5).

Yup, free comedy every Sunday lunchtime at The Stand. Banish your hangover and set off on the road to recovery with two hours of improvised sketches based entirely on audience suggestions. Lunch on laughs at this local institution (5 York Pl, New Town, t: 0131 558 7272, Map B3).

Old Money

For the true insider, Edinburgh offers more refined luxury than a period drama. Status and bloodlines can open doors that are closed to most mortals. For those that have neither, a good reference and the right bank account might just be the passport.

Step into another age by joining the exclusive Drumsheugh Baths, Edinburgh's oldest private swimming club. This Moorish style building was completed in 1822 and is geared up for the perfect Victorian workout, with Roman Rings and trapeze hanging over the pool (5 Belford Rd, West End, t: 0131 225 2200, beyond Map D4).

The city once had dozens of private clubs, and The New Club is one of the oldest surviving examples. If Phileas Fogg had set out from Edinburgh, this would have been his obvious point of departure. Founded in 1787, the club features the all essential card room and maintains some of its pre-modern rules (86 Princes St, New Town, t: 0131 226 4881, Map C4).

There are over 40 private gardens dotted around the city's most expensive postal addresses. Ownership of a grand house or apartment will grant residents the magical key to Edinburgh's stunning and secretive green spaces. Some will allow non-neighbours to apply for a key but for a fee. Try your luck with Merchiston Garden, Regent Gardens (Map A3) or Dean Gardens (Map D3).

Edinburgh's private gardens have an annual open doors day in May; historical buildings (private or public) open for a day only in September. For details on open access days see www.cockburnassociation.org.uk

Tim Bell

The Port O'Leith Bar,
58 Constitution St, Leith,
beyond Map A1.

Trinity House Maritime Museum,
99 Kirkgate, Leith. Visits must be
pre-booked, call 0131 554 3289,
beyond Map A1.

Malcolm Fraser

Braid Hills No. 2 Course, 15 Braid Hills
Approach, call 0131 447 6666 to book a
tee time, 4 miles from city centre.

The Shore Bar, 3 Shore, Leith, beyond
Map A1.

Bennets Bar, 8 Leven St, Tollcross,
Map C6.

Clarks Bar, 142 Dundas St, New Town,
Map C2.

The Waverley, 3-5 St Mary's St, Old Town,
Map A4.

Botanic Gardens,
20a Inverleith Row, Inverleith, Map C1/D2.

Scott Monument, Princes St, New Town
Map B4.

The Outsider,
15-16 George IV Bridge, Old Town,
t: 0131 226 3131, Map B5.

Pizza Express,
1 Deanhaugh St, Stockbridge,
t: 0131 332 7229, Map D3.

Marina's Café, 61 Cockburn St,
Old Town, Map B4.

Outlook Tower, Castlehill, Old Town,
Map B4.

Glenogle Baths,
Glenogle Rd, Stockbridge, Map D2.

Gavin Hastings

Murrayfield Stadium, Murrayfield.
For tours book 48 hours in advance,
t: 0131 346 5100, 2 miles from
city centre.

Murrayfield Hotel, 18 Corstorphine Rd,
Murrayfield, 2 miles from city centre.

Roseburn Bar, 1 Roseburn Terrace,
Murrayfield, 2 miles from city centre

Café Royal Circle Bar, 17 West
Register St, off east end of Princes St,
Map B4.

Run Costorphine Hill, enter via a little
gate on Costorphine Rd, opposite the
intersection with Balgreen Rd, 2.5 miles
from city centre.

Run to Ratho Village by the Union
Canal (approx. 8 miles). Canal starts at
Fountainbridge, Map D6.

The Bridge Inn Pub in Ratho Village
organises Sunday lunch cruises in the
canal. Barge also available for private hire,
t: 0131 333 1320 to book, 8 miles from
city centre.

Bob McCulloch

The Patio, 87 Hanover St, New Town,
t: 0131 226 3653, Map B4.

La Partenope, 96 Dalry Rd, off Haymarket,
t: 0131 347 8880, beyond Map D5.

Black Medicine Coffee Co,
2 Nicolson St, Old Town, Map A5.

Valvona & Crolla, 19 Elm Row,
Leith Walk, Map A3.

The Deacon's House, 3 Brodies Close,
304 Lawnmarket, Old Town, Map B4.

The Montgomery Fish Bar,
5-7 Montgomery St off the top of
Leith Walk, Map A3.

Sandy Bell's, 25 Forrest Rd,
Old Town, Map B5.

Canny Man's, 237 Morningside Rd,
Morningside, Map D8.

The Wide Awake Club, for early birds only!

David Ramsden

The Kitchin, 78 Commercial Quay,
Leith. Open tue-sat, t: 0131 555 1755,
beyond Map A1.

Himalaya Tandoori Restaurant,
171 Bruntsfield Pl, Brunstfield,
t: 0131 229 8216, Map D7.

Spoon Café, 15 Blackfriars St,
Old Town, Map A4.

The Farmer's Market,
every Saturday 9am-2pm on
Castle Terrace, Map C5.

Blackford Hill, by Morningside,
south of the city centre.
(See also Beautiful Walks section)

Anna & Mike

Dusit, 49a Thistle St, New Town,
t: 0131 220 6846, Map C4.

Harvey Nichols Fourth Floor Restaurant,
30-34 St Andrews Sq, New Town,
t: 0131 524 8350, Map B3.

Tigerlily, 125 George St, New Town,
t: 0131 225 5005, Map C4.

The Manna House, 22-24 Easter Rd,
Beyond Map A3.

The Union of Communication Workers,
15 Brunswick St, near top of
Leith Walk, Map A3.

DesignShop, 116 Causewayside,
Southside, Map A7.

Mary Contini

*The Royal College of Surgeons'
Museum,* Nicolson St, Old Town,
open mon-fri, noon-4pm,
Map A5.

The Edinburgh Room at the
Central Library, George IV Bridge,
Old Town, open mon-sat, Map B5.

The Dean Gallery, 75 Belford Rd,
near Dean Village, beyond Map D4.

The Church of Our Lady of Loretto,
Musselburgh (7 miles from Edinburgh),
take bus 15 from Princes St.

Inveresk Lodge Gardens, 24 Inveresk
Village, Musselburgh (7 miles from
Edinburgh), take bus 44 or 26, open all
year 10am-6pm or dusk if earlier.

Nick Thorpe

The Edinburgh Canal Society at the
Union Canal, off Ashley Terrace,
Sundays only, from 11am to 5pm,
weather permitting, beyond Map D8.

Waterstone's Bookshop,
128 Princes St, West End, Map C4.

Caffé Lucano, 37-39 George IV Bridge, Old Town, Map B5.

The John Murray Archive Exhibition at the National Library of Scotland, George IV Bridge, Old Town, Map B5.

The Socrates Café, every second Sunday of the month, The Filmhouse Cinema, 88 Lothian Rd, Map C5.

Newhaven Harbour and The Old Chain Pier, 32 Trinity Crescent, Newhaven (take bus 10 bus from Princes St), 2.5 miles from city centre.

Jude Doherty

Barony Bar, 81-85 Broughton St, New Town Map B3.

Teuchters, 26 William St, West End, Map D4.

The Oxford Bar, 8 Young St, New Town, Map C4.

Thistle Street Bar, 39 Thistle St, New Town, Map C4.

King's Wark, 36 Shore, Leith, beyond Map A1.

The Shore Bar, 3 Shore, Leith, beyond Map A1.

Fiona Donegan

Black Bo's, 57 Blackfriar's St, off the Royal Mile, Old Town, Map A4.

Wildfire, 192 Rose St, New Town, t: 0131 225 3636, Map C4.

The Bongo Club, 37 Holyrood Rd, Old Town, Map A4.

John Croall

Queen's Gallery at the Palace of Holyroodhouse, Canongate, beyond Map A4.

Edinburgh Folk Club, Wednesdays 7.30pm, Pleasance Cabaret Bar, 60 The Pleasance, Southside, t: 0131 650 2349, check www.edinburghfolkclub.org.uk for listings, closes for August, Map A5.

Links Tavern, 5-7 Restalrig Rd off Leith Links, Leith, beyond Map A2.

Sandy Bell's, 25 Forrest Rd, Old Town, Map B5.

Domenico's, 30 Sandport St, Leith, beyond Map A1.

Trendy Wendy

HMV, 129 Princes St, New Town, Map C4.

Underground Solu'shun, 9 Cockburn St, Old Town, Map B4.

Fopp, 7 Rose St, New Town, Map B4.

The Red Door Gallery, 42 Victoria St, Old Town, Map B5.

Cabaret Voltaire, 36 Blair St, Old Town, Map A4.

Ego, 14 Picardy Place, New Town, Map A3.

Lulu, 125 George St, New Town, Map C4.

Hector's Bar, 47 Deanhaugh St, Stockbridge, Map D3.

Villager, 49-50 George IV Bridge, Old Town, t: 0131 226 2781, Map B5.

Amicus Apple, 17 Frederick St, New Town, Map C4.

The Witchery, Castlehill, Royal Mile, Old Town, t: 0131 225 5613, Map B4/5.

Ruth Kirkpatrick

Guid Crack, last Friday of the month at The Waverley Bar, 3-5 St Mary's St, Old Town, Map A4.

Céilidhs at ALP (Adult Learning Project), once a month at St Bride's Centre, Orwell Terrace, Haymarket. Go to www. alpscotsmusic.org/ceilidhs or call 0131 346 1405/555 7668 for details, beyond Map D5.

Steiner School Christmas Fair, Steiner School, 60/64 Spylaw Rd, near Morningside. Call for dates, t: 0131 337 3410, beyond Map D8.

Sadivino, 52 West Richmond St, Southside, t: 0131 667 7719, Map A5.

The Traquair Fayre in Traquair House (near Peebles), first weekend of August. From Edinburgh take bus 62 to Innerleithen (leaves from St Andrews Sq every hour) or drive for 29 miles.

Holly Campbell & Lynsey Miller

Antiques & Decorative Art Fair, Royal Highland Centre, Ingliston (near the airport).

Alan K.L Jackson, 67 Causewayside, Southside, t: 0131 668 4532, Map A6.

Sam Burn's Junk Yard, Cockenzie,

12 miles from Edinburgh.

Empire, 24 St. Mary's St, Old Town, t: 0131 466 0100, Map A4.

Dusit, 49a Thistle St, New Town. t: 0131 220 6846, Map C4.

Villager, 49-50 George IV Bridge, Old Town, t: 0131 226 2781, Map B5.

Urban Angel, 121 Hanover St, New Town, t: 0131 225 6215, Map C3.

Ride This Train at *The Bongo Club,* 37 Holyrood Rd, Old Town. Check www.myspace.com/ridethistrainclub for details, Map A4.

Citrus Club, 40-42 Grindlay St, off Lothian Rd, Map C5.

Megabowl, Fountainbridge Park, Map D6.

The Sheep Heid Inn, 43-45 The Causeway, Duddingston Village (30 mins from the foot of Arthur's Seat). Call 0131 656 6951 to book the skittle alley.

Lisa

Murrayfield Ice Rink, Riversdale Crescent, Murrayfield, t: 0131 337 6933, 2 miles from city centre. From 2.30pm on weekdays, from 10.00am on weekends.

Paperchase, 77a George St, New Town, Map C4.

Waterstone's Booksellers, 83 George St, New Town, Map C4.

The National Museum of Scotland, Chambers St, Old Town, Map B5.

The Museum of Childhood, 42 High St (Royal Mile), Old Town, Map A4.

hank you All Thank you All Thank yo

A big thank you to Claire Dowling for adjusting to impossible deadlines and having the passion to turn abstract ideas into beautiful, truly original images (www.clairedowling.com). Thank you to Matt Reid for his enthusiasm, eye for detail and for always capturing the spirit of places and people. (matthewjamesreid@yahoo.co.uk). Dear reader: if you're one of those people who commissions design and photography work do not hesitate to hire them. They're very special. Thanks to all the locals who shared their tips and time with us: Gavin Hastings (extra thanks for your very Scottish attitude to the ever changeable weather), Jude Doherty, Bob McCulloch, Mary Contini, Trendy Wendy, David Ramsden, Nick Thorpe, Ruth Kirkpatrick, John Croall, Lisa (and Alison), Anna and Mike Christopherson, Holly Campbell (to whom we were, literally, a pain) and Lynsey Miller, Malcolm Fraser, Tim Bell and Fiona Donegan.

Thanks to all of our contributors, particularly Andy Meldrum whose extensive knowledge of his home city uncovered countless gems mentioned in these pages. Thanks also to old romantic Keith McGilivray, charity shop cruiser Fiona McCurdy, canal queen Rebecca Chapman, Easter Road experts Eilidh Slimon and Brendan Grigg, sweet tooth Fiona Muir, Italian foodie Tracy Scodellaro, girl with the gift Rebecca Peppiette, Tollcross tipster Kerryn Hurley, Dance Base diva James Allenby, Farmer's Market fanatic Martha Bryce, Monster Mash man Dave Elcock, labyrinth lady Sheila Harrison, Le Monde legend Jamie Corr, the happiest man in Edinburgh - Kevin Malone, whose new pub pact led us to so many undiscovered drinking dens. And Emer O'Leary who introduced Owen to the greatest city in the world and who continues to find us more and more reasons to enjoy living here.

Thanks to everyone who imparted advice, some brain power and (even) kit: Séan Costello and John McColgan for a window on the world of publishing; Rob Wilson for lending his brand new tripod; Anna and Ali at Edinburgh City of Literature for solving so many of our literary conundrums; Catherine Lockerbie and James Shaw at the Book Festival for bouncing ideas on books; Martin Wishart for the lovely (and very Scottish) recipe; Robert King for printing satin labels; Lizzie MacGregor at the Scottish Poetry Library for suggesting poems, Maggie Scott at Scottish Language Dictionaries for telling us how today's weather is written with yesterday's words.

Thank you All Thank you All Thank

Thanks to Susan Chang, Sang Kim, Rory and Sue Costello in New York, Rick Heffernan and Christina Valente in Barcelona, Miki Iwane, Padraig O'Brien and Daire Moynihan in London, Fergal Collins in Dublin, Kenton, Cristina, Stacey and João in Lisbon and everybody in cities across the world who have acted as the perfect local hosts inspiring this guide.

Cheers to all the enthusiastic flickr members who so kindly gave us permission to reproduce their amazing photographs: Rachel Cowan (flickr user: curlsdiva, page 68), David Ross (flickr user: davydubbit, page 26), Lindsay Perth (www.lippi. org, page 79), David Harding (flickr user: davidcharding, page 35), Paul Davidson (flickr user: elementalPaul, page 71, 130), Stewart Hardy (flickr user: Semi-detached, page 15).

Thanks to Paula Kennedy for her beautiful handwriting and her illustration on page 103 (www.paula-kennedy.com) and to Mina Braun for her magical drawing on page 107 (www.minabraun.com).

Thanks to Scrabble hero Peggy Hughes for bringing her eagle eyes into the proofing process. Thanks also to Ken McCallum and his team at Scotprint for all their time and advice.

Thanks to Habitat and Megabowl Fountainbridge for lending props for the portraits; the appreciation is extended to all managers of locations for co-operating with our photo shoots.

Claudia does not have enough words to say thank you thank you thank you to Ian, for his belief and support when she could only talk travel guides. She hopes to return that kind of royal treatment one day, perhaps with some subzero mighty turns.

Owen has plenty of words (gone unsaid) for the beautiful girl in the bar whose conversation was cut short for a late night proofing session. He's sure it was wroth it.

Too good to leave out

I scream you scream
We all scream for ice cream! Lothian's Luca's stocks Irn Bru ice cream amongst others. Need we say any more?
(16 Morningside Rd, Morningside, Map D7)

A close shave
Victoria the Turkish Barbers on Leith Walk are renowned for the best shave in the city. Let's see your face in the place!
(3 Haddington Pl, Leith Walk, Map A3)

Smokin'
Something Fishy stocks the finest smoked salmon in the city. Smoked on the premises and tastier than anywhere else, don't let it be the one to get away!
(16a Broughton St, New Town, Map A3)

An Eskimo walks into a bar
The barman says 'Welcome to Iglu'. Use your Inuit-ion and get down to this cosy cool compact pub.
(2b Jamaica St, New Town, Map C3)

Too good to forget

Know even better spots in the city?
Have your say and email your recommendations to
toptips@localsguidetoedinburgh.com

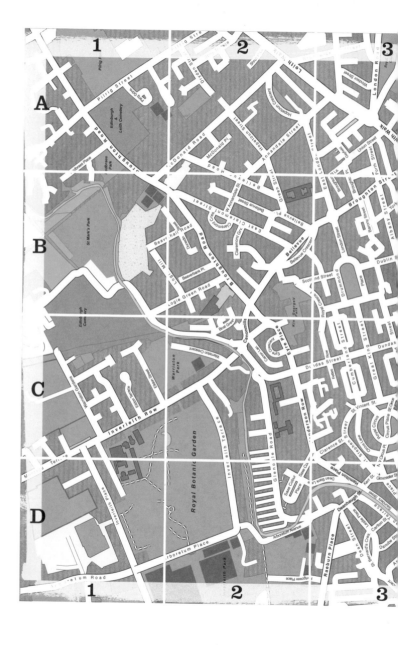